php|architect's Guide to Programming Magento

by Mark Kimsal

php|architect's Guide to Programming Magento

First Edition: May 2008

ISBN: **978-0-9738621-7-1**

Produced in Canada

Printed in the United States

Disclaimer

Written by	Mark Kimsal
Published by	Marco Tabini & Associates, Inc.
	28 Bombay Ave.
	Toronto, ON M3H 1B7
	Canada
	(416) 630-6202 / (877) 630-6202
	info@phparch.com / www.phparch.com
Publisher	Marco Tabini
Technical Reviewer	Paul Reinheimer
Layout and Design	Arbi Arzoumani
Managing Editor	Elizabeth Naramore
Finance and Resource Management	Emanuela Corso

Contents

Chapter 1

Introduction

E-commerce programming represents what is probably the most creative outlet for a developer. Implementing an e-commerce solution for yourself, or for a client, requires creative solutions to stay one step ahead of your competitors in the ever-changing online world. Enticing potential customers to "turn-over" and become customers of your store calls for the best user experience. Organization, searching, fast load times, attractive display, and intuitive navigation must all come together to form a shopping experience that builds a level of trust between your store and the customer. Starting an e-commerce solution with the absolute best tools gives you a solid foundation on which to try out your customer-enticing ideas. Starting with less than adequate tools creates artificial and time wasting barriers between you and your ultimate goal: enticing customers to buy from you.

Starting an e-commerce solution with Magento gives you the best possible foundation for your online Web store. Whether you know a little or a lot about programming, you will see how Magento offers you the best programming platform to flex your creative mind. From minute template controls to custom modules, to exclusive product behaviors, Magento can help you finish an implementation faster than the alternatives.

Who Can Use This Book?

Developers

This book should serve as a thorough introduction for developers to the structure of Magento, as well as provide you with enough examples that you can take any of your coding ideas to fruition. Developers will learn how to write custom modules for Magento for redistribution or for simply deploying on a corporate installation of Magento.

Store Owners

If you are not a programmer, but simply want to **run** a Magento store, this book might not be for you, but if you think you might need custom programming for your shopping cart this book can help you communicate better with your developers.

It's tough to avoid getting the wool pulled over your eyes when hiring a remote developer. Armed with the knowledge of Magento provided by this book, you should be able to verify any cost estimates you receive and find out if your developers are stalling or not.

About This Book

This book is organized roughly into two sections. The first section describes how Magento works from a code perspective and from a general user-interface perspective. The remaining chapters will walk the reader through building various *modules* for Magento by example. Although not a complete detail of Magento's API, this book should give the reader all the learning by examples that he or she should need to understand all the concepts that drive Magento's code.

Code Formatting

Since Magento is built on the Zend Framework the code formatting of the examples in this book will follow the Zend Framework style guidelines. Sometimes the code examples in this book are shortened to fit on the pages, so style may suffer in some instances to conserve space.

When referring to variables, classes, objects, or concepts this book will put the word or words in question into *italics*. When specifically referring to the word of a variable, class name, etc. the words will be formatted as inline `code`. File names will also be formatted this way.

When talking about *Mage_Core_Model_Abstract* the object class italics will be used, but when talking about why a class is named `Mage_Core_Model_Abstract`, inline code formatting will be used.

XML Examples

When referencing XML the ellipses, ..., are used to suggest that other, optional, or pre-existing XML tags are present. Given the XML structure below:

```xml
<config>
    <modules>
        <Company_RewardPoints>
            <version>0.1.0</version>
            <depends>
                <Mage_Customer />
                <Mage_Checkout />
            </depends>
        </Company_RewardPoints>
    </modules>
    <global>
        <resources>
            <rewardpoints_setup>
                <setup>
                    <module>Company_RewardPoints</module>
                    <class>Mage_Core_Model_Resource_Setup</class>
                </setup>
                <connection><use>core_setup</use></connection>
            </resources>
    </global>
</config>
```

The section enclosed in the `rewardpoints_setup` tag may be represented as this:

```xml
<config>
```

```
...
  <global>
...

        <resources>
           <rewardpoints_setup>
              <setup>
                 <module>Company_RewardPoints</module>
                 <class>Mage_Core_Model_Resource_Setup</class>
              </setup>
              <connection><use>core_setup</use></connection>
        </resources>
...
  </global>
...
</config>
```

Operating System Considerations

When possible, this book will describe technical procedures for Linux, Mac OS X, and Windows operating systems. However, to keep examples brief, simple references to file locations will use Windows directory and file naming conventions. When listing directories, the forward slash (/) will be used as a directory separator as this convention falls in line with standard Unix behavior (Mac OS X and Linux) plus PHP and Apache can automatically translate forward slashes to back slashes where need be on Windows.

```
Do not be surprised to see a directory like this:
C:/xampp/apache/htdocs/magento/
```

Chapter 2

Developing for Magento

Prep Your Environment

Make sure you have the most up-to-date version of Magento downloaded.

Start by downloading the latest release of Magento from `http://magentocommerce.com/`.

LAMP/WAMP Platform

If you are on the Windows platform the easiest way to install PHP, Apache and MySQL is with the XAMPP family of packages from `http://apachefriends.org`. Install the XAMPP-lite package anywhere on your drive and run the `setup.bat` file. There is a version of XAMPP for Mac OS X and Linux as well.

Subversion

For developing your own modules, it is recommended that you use Subversion version control to keep track of all of your code changes. TortoiseSVN from `http://tortoisesvn.tigris.org` is the recommended client and server for Windows users. For Mac and Linux users, the command line `svn` program plus the PHP package *websvn* is recommended. If you are not familiar with the Subversion system, you can read more about it at the Subversion Web site (`http://subversion.tigris.org/`).

MySQL Tools

Apart from the actual MySQL server, it is most useful to have a graphical client to inspect Magento's database tables from time to time. The *MySQL Query Browser* tool is the official client provided by MySQL AB and is available for all major operating systems. Some users prefer *mysqlcc* or *phpMyAdmin* over *MySQL Query Browser*, though.

Installation

Unzip Magento into your Web server's document root (from here on, referenced as *{docroot}*). You should see a directory layout like this:

```
{docroot}/magento/
                app/
                index.php
                js/
                lib/
                LICENSE.txt
                media/
                pear
                skin/
                var/
```

Database Setup

Magento will not create its required database for you, even if your database user has proper rights to create a database. Because of this, we will need to create the database using one of the previously mentioned MySQL tools. A normal database name, sometimes called a *schema*, can be "magento", or "magento_dev", or you can even include the version number "magento_10".

Magento Setup

You should now continue with Magento's base installation by pointing your browser to http://localhost/magento/. Here, you will see a basic step-by-step form for installing most PHP Web applications. Follow the on-screen directions and your Magento installation will be complete.

Sample Data

If this is your first time trying out Magento you should install the optional sample data. The sample data is provided as a separate download as it is about 35 MB. The sample data provides some sample products, categories, and product images. Once you have downloaded the package, copy the `media` folder over your own `media` folder under your Magento installation. Then run the provided SQL file with your MySQL management tool.

As of the time of this writing, the sample data is distributed as a complete database installation. Therefore, it needs to be inserted before you proceed with the regular setup. The regular setup will actually **upgrade** the sample data to the latest version.

Initializing Subversion

Magento has three directories from which modules are executed: `core`, `community`, and `local`. All the examples in this book assume that you are developing in the `local` module directory. Under the `local` directory, you can group all of your modules together under one package. This package is called `Mage` for all magento core modules, but this book will use `Company` for all the examples. You can use any package name besides `Company` for a package name that represents your company or organization.

Initializing subversion is a bit tricky. First, you need to initialize a repository. Then, you need to create a folder or directory to import into this new repository. After that you are **not** ready to start using subversion. The directory which was imported needs to be removed, and then `checked out` of the repository in order for it to be connected with subversion. Let's look at the steps in detail.

Picking a subversion repository on the Linux platform is pretty easy. After installing Subversion from RPM, there usually exists a directory similar to `/var/lib/subversion/repositories/`. Initialize a new repository with the command:

```
svnadmin create /var/lib/subversion/repositories/magento_modules
```

If you are using TortoiseSVN under Windows, create a folder anywhere on your computer, right-click that folder, and select `Create repository here...` from the TortoiseSVN menu.

Our goal for setting up Subversion is to have a folder named `Company` under the `app/code/local` directory of Magento. This will allow us to easily add new modules and save our work to Subversion whenever we want. Create a new directory under the `app/code/local` folder called `svn_import`. Under this temporary `svn_import` directory create another folder called `Company`, or whichever name you've decided to use for your packaging. If you are running on a Unix platform, run this command from *inside* the svn_import directory (ignoring the shell prompt):

```
[svn_import]$ svn import . \
   file:///var/lib/svn/repositories/magento_modules/
```

On Windows, use TortoiseSVN by right-clicking on the `svn_import` folder and choosing the `Import...` menu item. A new dialog will appear and ask you to input the URL of the repository. Click the ellipses button and browse to the folder which you designated as your repository in the previous step.

Delete the `svn_import` folder after successfully importing into your new repository. Next, we need to *checkout* the folder we just imported to get a Subversion activated directory. On Unix:

```
[local]$ svn checkout \
    file:///var/lib/svn/repositories/magento_modules/Company
```

On Windows, right click on the `local` folder and choose `SVN Checkout...`. Accept the default settings in the dialog, and confirm `Yes` when it asks you if you really want to overwrite the folder.

Covering all Subversion commands is beyond the scope of this book. But you are now prepared to develop and save your custom Magento modules in a subversion directory if you so choose.

Chapter 3

Exploring Magento

Magento's administrative interface gives you control over all the standard features of your shopping cart site. Looking at this *backend* interface can shed some light on what features Magento has to offer. Login to the backend with the admin account which you setup during the installation and you will see something like the screen shown in Figure 3.1.

Figure 3.1

Magento provides standard functionality that you would expect from any shopping cart, including:

- Multiple category trees

- Definable attributes

- Customer and customer group management

- Discount rules for promotions

- Newsletter management

- Web page manager

- Order review system

- Reporting features

- System configuration and settings

In addition to these features, there are a number of features that would not be provided by default in other shopping carts. A short list of these impressive features include:

- Reviewing search terms

- Reviewing customer tags

- Poll manager

- Currency exchange rates

- Google Sitemap integration

- Abandoned shopping cart report

- Layered category navigation

None of these features by themselves are probably that impressive. But to have a system in which they are all present, by default, with no plugins necessary, is truly a breath of fresh air in the open source e-commerce arena.

By now, you've probably "clicked" around in the backend a little. The remainder of this chapter will guide you through the basics of what Magento has to offer and cover Magento specific terms. It is necessary to have a thorough understanding of Magento's basic operation in order to better understand the code. Let's start with Magento's *product catalog*.

Magento Catalogs

A product catalog is the combination of products that you wish to sell and those products' categorizations and pricing. You can equate this with any catalog you might receive in the mail. The pages are organized by category, the products have a description, a picture, a price, and some product code or number that you can use when placing an order. As you are flipping through the pages of the catalog, the catalog itself represents your entire view of that company's products. If, for some reason, the catalog is not organized correctly, or the product images seem unattractive, you might be quite inclined to toss the catalog to the side and not think about ordering from that company. Likewise, when a customer is browsing your e-commerce site, the product catalog is possibly their only view of you or your company.

Figure 3.2

As you can see from Figure 3.2, a *catalog*, in Magento, consists of categories, products, and attributes. A few other tools that Magento lumps into catalog maintenance are: URL rewrite management, search term review, customer product review, product tags, and Google Sitemap. While there are no direct relationships between these features and a physical, printed catalog, there is no doubt that all of these features contribute to the customer's overall view of your e-commerce site.

Categories

Categories are the most visible aspect of your catalog. The structure of the categories directly translates into navigation for the customer. A customer viewing your site store on a product display page, coming from either a search engine or from another link, will see the product's categorization as a *bread crumb* trail near the top of the page.

While a paper catalog is limited to the amount of pages that can be delivered to a potential customer, a digital catalog is not. Any product can be categorized under as many categories as it makes sense. Thankfully, Magento does allow for a product to be listed under multiple categories.

Start by clicking on the **Manage Categories** link under **Catalog** in the Magento backend. You will see the current categories listed as a nested folder tree. Selecting any category by clicking on it will reload the page and allow you to edit that category on the right side of the page. There are some fairly standard attributes of any category that you can edit, including: name, description, category image, `meta keywords`, etc. Magento specific features of categories include: CMS block, display mode, URL key, layout updates, and anchor mode.

CMS Blocks

Using a CMS block with a category allows you to go above and beyond a plain text description of your category. CMS blocks allow full HTML to be used inside them, as well as special Magento commands. The display mode allows you to turn on and off the listing of products, CMS blocks, or both for the front-end view of the category.

URL Key

The URL key, sometimes referred to as *SEO text* (Search Engine Optimization), gives you the opportunity to include any keywords that you wish to display in the URL for this category. By default, the URL key is taken from the name of the category, removing or replacing any characters that would not show well in a URL. You should use care when changing this value. Having special SEO words in your category URLs is great for search engine rankings, but if the words constantly change it might appear that you have too many distinct URLs pointing to one page. This might have the effect of lowering your rankings in certain search engines, or causing any indexing spider to stop indexing your site. This problem is well documented in various articles about SEO.

Layout Updates

There are two types of layout changes you can make for each category. The first is just a page layout change. This allows you to display your category with one of the pre-built page layouts. The basic page layouts are: 1 column, 2 columns with right bar, 2 columns with left bar, and 3 columns. This gives you the flexibility to turn on and off any content that would normally show up in the side columns, like the category menu or your shopping cart contents.

The other type of layout update is the "Custom Layout Update". This text box allows you to enter raw XML commands, exactly like those that power the layout system. We will talk more about the layout system later, but this feature is very powerful, allowing you to control almost any aspect of the final rendering of any category.

Anchor Mode

The *anchor mode* attribute is probably the worst named of all attributes in the system. For any category, setting *Is Anchor* to *Yes* will turn on the feature known as *layered navigation*. When a category is an anchor, the normal list of sub-categories that would appear when browsing that category is replaced by a set of attribute groups of all products contained in that category and below.

This new navigation control allows your customers to find products based on any available attribute of the products contained at or below the current category. A typical layered navigation panel might look something like this to the end user:

```
Shop By
- - - - - - - - - - - - - - - - - - - -
Category:
Digital Cameras (7)
Film Cameras (2)

Price:
$1-$100 (4)
$101-$200 (3)
$201-$400 (2)

Manufacturer:
Fuji (3)
Canon (3)
Olympus (3)
```

It is referred to as an "anchor" because the user no longer "moves" to lower sub-categories, instead the list of available products is merely filtered by the customer's chosen attributes. This is a very powerful feature and Magento might be the first to offer such a feature in an open source shopping cart.

Products

Products are the heart of any e-commerce site. But in Magento, they might be called another body part: the Achilles' heel. In Magento, the definition of a product is exceedingly simple. One *SKU* is one product that a customer can buy. The problem with Magento's product support is that you must create one SKU for each product that you want to sell. There is no SKU formula nor SKU pattern where selected options alter, or add to, an existing SKU for a base product. This can be problematic for manufacturers, handicraft artisans, printing shops, or anyone who wants to take instructions from the client. But, there are ways around this hiccup, that is why you are reading this book, no doubt. We will cover all the ways around this limitation.

Grouped Products

Grouped products provide the store owner with a way to collect many products and display them all on one product page. The products can be very similar to each other or loosely related, it doesn't matter. The grouped product type makes sense to use when you think the customer might want to purchase multiple different types of products at the same time. An example of this might be buying batteries: a typical customer might wish to add many different packs of batteries to their cart at the same time, the only difference being the standard size of the batteries (i.e. A, AA, C, etc.).

Configurable Products

Configurable products are similar to grouped products in that they both are a collection of simple products. But, configurable products try to represent only one end product to a customer. When you associate simple products with a configurable product, all the simple products must share a common attribute set. The similarities

Figure 3.3

and differences between the attribute values of the simple products form a choice for the customer.

The best example of a configurable product would be shirts or clothing. A customer thinks of a shirt with an interesting design on it as just one product which is availble in many sizes and colors. Store owners think about the inventory of each size and color combination of that shirt. The simple products represent the physical inventory of real shirts in different sizes and colors, the configurable product represents the **choice** of which shirt the customer wants.

When a user browses to a configurable product, they see a series of input boxes which allow them to choose available values of the configurable attributes.

Figure 3.4

Bundled Products

Bundled products are not yet available at the time of this writing. The idea for a bundle is similar to what most systems call a `kit`. A *bundled* product will be one product in the customer's shopping cart, but it will be made of a number of real SKUs in the system that are treated as one whole. This is different from configurable products in that the goal of a configurable product is to select one real product from a set of products with similar attributes. The goal of a bundle is to provide a discount for purchasing things as a set, or to track inventory for all of the parts that combine to create one product.

Selling a computer, monitor, mousepad, and printer all together as one package would be an example of the first goal of bundled products. Selling a wooden bird house which is composed of 5 pieces of wood, 2 bolts, 1 package of glue, etc... would be an example of the second goal of bundling. No customer wants to directly purchase your raw material in the second example, but someone might simply want one mousepad from the first example.

Attribute System

The attribute system in Magento consists of attributes and attribute sets. An *attribute set* is a named group of attributes and can be attached to any number or products and thus defines which attributes can be associated with a product. Defining an attribute set for each *class* of product that you wish to sell is another way to organize your products, since some of the import and export functions can be limited to all the products of a specific attribute set.

The *attributes* themselves, while technically advanced, offer limited flexibility from a store owner's point of view. Defining a new attribute for use in the system can be complex if you don't understand all of the properties presented to you. Items like *Scope* and *Unique Values* might not make immediate sense to the store owner who is creating a new attribute. Let's take a look at each attribute property in detail. Remember that when you are designing a new attribute, all of the options relate to the product as it exists in your inventory, not to the user interface that a customer might see.

Attribute Identifier

This small identifier is used as a code word for the attribute throughout the system. Sometimes this identifier is used in XML, so don't use too many strange characters when naming it.

Scope

This allows you to specify how *far* any values of an attribute will spread in the system. If you are selling a product in multiple stores and you want each store to have one unique value for this attribute, then choose "Store View". We haven't discussed multiple stores yet, but if you imagine a Web site that sells to both American and European customers, you might want the "length" attribute to only have a "Store View" scope. That way, when you change the value to "12 inches" for the American store, the same product will keep any previous value for the European store, like "30 cm". Rarely would you ever want a value other than "Global" here.

Catalog Input Type for Store Owner

This allows you to select what sort of form control is present when you are editing your product inventory. This does not affect any visual form controls for the customer view. Most of the time it is sufficient to say "Dropdown". Using a dropdown control allows the attribute designer to list all possible values for this attribute, thereby reducing human error when editing the field.

Unique Value

If set to "Yes", this field will not allow you to have more than one product with the same value as another product using the same attribute. Think of this attribute like a license plate number, no two cars can have the same plate number at the same time.

Values Required

This property simply forces the store owner, or whoever is inputting the product data, to enter some value for this attribute when creating or editing a product. If set to "No" it allows the data entry person to skip over this attribute and leave it blank.

Input Validation for Store Owner

This property will run the store owner's data entry through a validation routine before saving the product data. Selecting "Dropdown" from the input type negates the value of this field.

Apply To

"*Apply To*" lets you specify that an attribute should behave differently if attached to a **Configurable** or **Grouped** product. If you are making an attribute that is the deciding factor between many of the same products (think size and color for shirts), then you will want to apply this attribute to a grouped or configurable product.

Multiple Stores

Magento only allows you to have one product catalog. This seems antithetical to what most people would want in an advanced shopping cart. But, what most systems would call a *catalog*, Magento calls a *store*. Each store can have its own root category, thus slicing the entire list of categories into many independent category trees. On the other hand, each category can have different products and settings for each store view. So it is up to you to decide whether reusing a category structure is useful for your situation when dealing with multiple stores.

To manage your stores, store views, and Web sites, login to the administrative back-end and click the Manage Stores link under the System tab. Here you can add new stores or store views. You can also rename a store or store view, but this only has an effect on the various controls of the admin interface, not the customer facing front-end. After you have created more than one store or store view you will see a store switcher widget on most of the admin interface pages. Selecting different store views in this drop-down menu will refresh the screen you're current viewing and allow you to make changes to values that will affect only the current store or store view.

Languages

After adding another *store view* to your site, you are allowed to enter alternative text to categories, products, and product attributes for each store view. If you have multiple stores installed you will see a special store view box on most admin pages. This box allows you to change values for a specific store view instead of the default values for products or categories. If you haven't specified any new values for the new store view, the view will take all of its values from the default store view. This is the most common way to run a store in multiple languages.

Figure 3.5 shows the *store view switcher* on the categories page to allow for changing values of a category only for one store view. The store switcher is also available for products, attributes, and general configurations when you have created more than one store view.

Figure 3.5

Multiple Catalogs

With Magento, you can create two completely separate product catalogs and basically run two separate stores from one installation. The trick involves creating a new *store*, not a store view. When you create a new store, you are allowed to choose which category is the root category for that store. Any product category whose parent is the *Root Category* is available to use as your new store's root category. These new categories will not be visible by anyone browsing a the original store.

There is no automatic way to activate the new store, however. Small changes to the index.php file are required if you wish to have a dynamic site which selects different stores at run-time. If you are running two different domain names, it might be easiest to install Magento once under each virtual host and simply enter in the same database settings into both installations.

Making the index file dynamically select a store view at run-time can be done a number of different ways and is heavily dependent on your particular situation. The core of the matter revolves around one line in the index.php file:

```
Mage::run();
```

The run method can accept the name of a *store view* as a parameter. You can simply type in the code name for your store and all hits to the Web site will use that store. A more sophisticated approach might be to inspect which sub-domain the customer has accessed the site with and pass that value to the run method. Another approach would be to inspect the customer's IP and try to geo-locate their country of origin, or simply inspect the browser's headers for the Accept-Language line.

```
if (stristr($_SERVER['HTTP_ACCEPT_LANGUAGE'],
            'zh-cn') !== false)
{
    $storecode = 'chinese';
} else {
    $storecode = 'default';
}
Mage::run($storecode);
```

Multiple Designs

If you are running multiple stores, you probably want to have multiple designs. For multi-language sites it is almost a requirement, since some of the Web site's assets will no doubt have language directly written on graphics or logos. Magento's concept of designs is split up into two ideas: packages and themes. Packages are a complete rewrite of every single part of Magento's front-end, and are usually over-kill unless you know that your project will radically alter how products are shown to the customer.

Using different themes in the same design package allows a fine-grained approach to tweaking Magento's layout, graphics and CSS files. A theme is physically a new folder under a design package folder. Themes have the advantage of falling back to the default theme folder if a certain template, graphic, or CSS file is not found in the custom theme. Custom packages do not fall back to the default package if a file is missing.

Different themes can be applied to a single category, an entire branch of categories, or to a new store or store view. Applying themes to individual categories is useful for different promotional or advertising needs, but it is probably not a good approach for managing design changes for internationalization needs.

Chapter 4

Magento Modules

Modules are the core of Magento. Every action on the site, frontend or backend, goes through a module. Modules act as containers for one or more of the following: settings, database schemas, rendering objects, utility helpers, data models, or action controllers. A module can be made of all six of these things, or just one. Modules are defined as being on or off in an XML configuration system located in app/etc/modules/. Each module can specify its own settings in an XML file as well, located under the module's etc/ directory.

Since everything in Magento is a module, and modules have self-contained configuration and database settings, this allows you, as a developer, to extend Magento exactly as the core system is built.

Module Structure

Below you can see the directory structure of the *Catalog* module. The catalog module contains all of the aspects of a module.

```
- Mage/
  |- Catalog/
  |   |- Block/
  |   |- Helper/
  |   |- Model/
  |   |- controllers/
```

```
|   |- etc/
|    - sql/
```

Code Pools

Modules are located in one of three *code pools*. The code pools are: core, local, and community. All of the modules distributed with the base Magento are in the core code pool. All of the custom modules that you develop can be installed in the local code pool. The community pool was originally designed for installed third-party modules, but this idea might be phased out, as you can simply install any module in local as well as community.

```
- app/
  - code/
    |- local/
    |- community/
     - core/
```

Module Packages

All models exist under a package directory. The package serves no purpose other than to allow for consistent naming of classes. All Magento modules are part of the Mage package. Thus, all Magento class names begin with Mage_. It is an acceptable practice to create a new package for your custom modules that has the name of your company or organization instead of Mage. There is no functional detriment when not using Mage as your package.

Models

Models are the muscle of Magento. They help move data from the database into the program itself. The output, or rendering, of the data is done by the Blocks, but the models are mainly responsible for manipulating the data. Models, in any programming environment, help to identify and shape data domains. What this means is that models draw boundaries between definitions of data groups and relate data groups to other data groups.

To help illustrate the idea of data modeling imagine creating a shopping cart system and that you want to have a *Product* class. This product should have an image associated with it. But, the question is, how does that image get *modeled*? Do you simply give the product one $image_url variable? Perhaps it is best to link the Product class to an Image_Gallery class and create linking methods between the two, e.g. getDefaultImage. The resulting model classes are the end result of your decision on how the data interrelates.

Blocks

Blocks are the brains behind Magento's templating scheme. Blocks form a nested set of objects that coordinate the models with the template files. Each block controls one template file: a simple HTML and PHP mixed file with a .phtml extension. What this means is that for any page request on Magento, you are dealing with an equal, but large, number of Block objects and .phtml template files.

All blocks extend the base class Mage_Core_Block_Template, which, in turn, extends Mage_Core_Block_Abstract. The chief method of a block is its toHtml() method. This method translates the block's template file into HTML using the renderView() method.

Magento's template system is just plain PHP. They don't re-implement any other templating system, so the renderView() method simply does an include() on the requested .phtml template file. If, in fact, you wanted to add a different templating mechanism into Magento, the Mage_Core_Block_Template class's renderView method is where you would trigger your chosen template system's rendering functions.

Controllers

Controllers are the starting point for all business logic in Magento. The line between what is considered business logic (rules that define a business's methodology) and what is domain logic (instructions about a set of data) is blurry in Magento. Some people would consider checking for required and optional form fields as "business logic", other people would consider that "domain logic". Most of the logic in Magento is done in the *models*.

Controllers extend a base class of `Mage_Core_Controller_Varien_Action`, which is a close copy of the Zend Framework class `Zend_Controller_Action`. The important methods of this class are:

- dispatch($action)

- preDispatch()

- postDispatch()

The rest of the methods are simply utility URLs to pass commands to other key parts of the system. The `dispatch` method starts all the business logic of the current request. The value of `$action` is determined from the URL and is generally "index" as a default. The `dispatch` method first calls `preDispatch` which triggers some events which you can listen for:

- controller_action_predispatch

- controller_action_predispatch_ModuleName

- controller_action_predispatch_ModuleName_ControllerName_ActionName

The `dispatch` method is called only if the `preDispatch` method does not mark the request as being **dispatched** already. The `dispatch` method calls the particular action method in the desired controller instance (Figure 4.1).

Helpers

Helpers in Magento are simply a way to abstract (or refactor) utility methods out of core classes. Most access to helpers are doubly wrapped up inside various *Block* and *Model* methods anyway, so the value of helpers is pretty dubious. Very rarely do you want to override or sub-class a helper. It is very easy to simply add a new helper to provide additional utility functionality to your scripts.

The two major methods of helpers that you should be interested in are:

- __ (just two underscores)

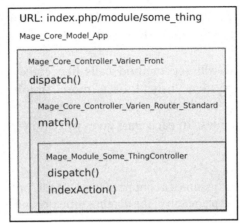

Figure 4.1

- *htmlEscape*

The double underscore method `__` is a translation helper. This helper function is wrapped from almost any object context, which means you can safely call `$this->__('My English Text')` at almost any point in your code to translate a string. The `htmlEscape` function simply wraps PHP's native `htmlspecialchars` function, but it can also accept an array of data and escape each item individually.

Config files

Module configuration files are found in the `etc` folder under a module's main directory. There are 3 different config files available, all of which are XML. The only config file that directly affects your module's behavior is `config.xml`. The other two, `system.xml` and `convert.xml`, automatically create some setting forms for you on the system's main backend configuration page.

The contents of all modules' config files are merged into one massive collection of settings. This means that you can override the settings of any module in any other module simply by putting in the correct XML tags. This is the essence of overriding in Magento.

You can create any class for any purpose, and to install it into the system you create a new `config.xml` that specifies your class name in the same spot where the original class was defined.

This is also why you will see method calls like `getModel('catalog/product')` used throughout the system instead of a more simple approach like: `new Catalog_Model_Product()`.

The use of "tags", or names, for each class gives you a powerful way to override any part of the system.

> The use of tags for classes assumes a context of Block, Model or Helper. See the **Quick Answers** chapter for an explanation of the naming structure and how `catalog/product` translates into a real class name.

Template System

The template system in Magento is pretty controversial. The choice of using regular PHP for the templating language has caught some criticism from a few users. But, the choice of regular PHP has not made the templating system simple or under-powered, not by a long shot. This has to be the most flexible and advanced templating system that this author has ever seen (in PHP).

A complete page is rendered as a nested set of template files (technically, a nested set of *Blocks*). There are no explicit "widgets" in the system, that means, you won't find a specific "Form" class nor "Button" class or object. The lowly *Block* classes straddle the line between widgets and templates. The nested set of templates and blocks is controlled by... you guessed it, an XML file, specifically a set of XML files. This is quite powerful for developers and plug-in contributors, but it seems that it is overly complicated for most designers (even those familiar with PHP et al.).

Layout Files

The layout files control the structure of any final page rendering. They are located in the `layout` folder under your design theme. There are a number of XML files whose names loosely relate to an individual module, but they are all lower-case letters,

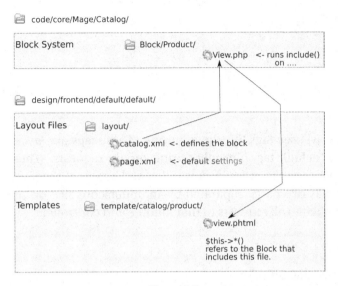

Figure 4.2

whereas the module names traditionally use the so-called `camel-case` method. The most important XML file is `page.xml`.

```
app/design/frontend/default/default/layout/
    ...
    page.xml
    catalogsearch.xml
    catalog.xml
    checkout.xml
    cms.xml
    contacts.xml
    ...
```

The `page.xml` file specifies the default page structure. All modifications from any of the other XML files are modifications of settings under the `default` XML tag. The following is a list of tags that are common to all layout files.

- layout

- default

- reference

- block

- action

- update

Sometimes you will see tags like the following. These tags are *layout handles,* they behave like the default tag, but only during certain requests. These tags follow a pattern that relates to the module, controller, and action of the given Web request. If the tag only has two parts, separated by an underscore, like `cms_page`, then these settings are applied to all requests to that module and controller.

- cms_page

- cms_index_defaultindex

- cms_index_defaultnoroute

- customer_account_index

- tag_customer_view

- catalog_product_view

Template Files

There's not much to say about the template files, they are simply plain PHP + HTML files that end in `.phtml` extension. The syntax used in these files tries to use the templating language features of PHP's syntax. You will see PHP's alternate loop structure syntax, which utilizes the colon (`:`) and `endwhile`, `endfor`, and `endif`, a lot in these files. Until recently, short tags were used throughout the template files, but all these have now been expanded to full PHP open tags plus the word `echo` where appropriate.

The structure of the directories mimics the structure of the corresponding modules, but it does not have to. This author has found that, when building your own custom modules, it is much easier to manage the files if you break convention and keep all your template files in one directory. You can do this by simply replacing slashes with underscores in your filename, thereby mimicking the original filename and directory structure. The worth of this advice is dependent on the size and scope of your custom modules. If you are overriding a small number of files, anywhere from one to fifty, the ability to instantly see which files are overridden by having them all in one directory is definitely beneficial.

There are a few important template files with which you should familiarize yourself. All of these files are located under the page sub-directory. The .phtml files in this directory are the highest level of change you can apply to any page. They grant 1, 2, or 3 column structure to any page, as well as providing "dashboard" type pages and a printer-friendly layout.

Although you can add any top-level template files in the page directory to your own theme, the default files are the only choice available to you via the admin interface. Let's say that you want a 4-column layout, so you create 4column.phtml. This 4column.phtml file will not be available to you in the admin interface as a setting for any CMS page. You can, however, switch the top-level file to your new 4column.phtml file or any other file that you make with XML settings in the layout files. So, this limitation is only a user interface limitation.

This book will focus on the application developer's needs and will only discuss the layout and template system to address the programmatic challenges of dealing with that system. For a designer's view of Magento's template system, read the design guide on http://magentocommerce.com//.

Mage Application

What happens in the code when you *hit* any given page in Magento? If you start by looking in the index.php file you will see that it is pretty light on code and documentation. The index file simply loads up the app/Mage.php file and tells it to run the "default" store.

```
//important contents of the index.php file

$mageFilename = 'app/Mage.php';
// [snip]
require_once $mageFilename;
```

```
umask(0);
Mage::run('default');
```

This Mage::run() method is simply a wrapper for 3 things: loading extensions, loading the App model, and running the **M**odel **V**iew **C**ontroller (MVC) style front controller (front "actions"). Any exceptions that make it this far up the execution stack are handled by first checking that Magento is completely installed, and, if so, printed to the screen. If Magento has not been installed any exception is treated as a signal that the installer needs to be run.

Magento's Request Cycle

Now we will discuss how a browser request to a URL gets translated into module execution. Generally speaking, any URL can be deconstructed like this:

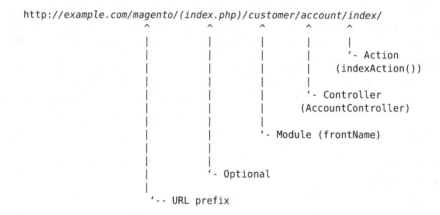

Magento's request cycle can be a little confusing to trace through. This is mostly due to the hierarchical nature of the file nesting (routers located under controllers) and the use of the term "**dispatch**" to mean 3 different things. The front controller "dispatches" the request to its internal list of "*routers*" and determines if any of the routers "*match()*" the request's parameters. If so, then a new MVC Controller (not front-controller) is created from the matching module and, again, the request is "**dispatched**" to this controller object. The final MVC-style controller is technically a "*Front Action*", it houses a number of methods that define the business logic tier. This new Action object dynamically calls one of its own *action* methods and marks the request as being "**dispatched**" (i.e. finished). All these uses of "dispatch" are still different from the event mechanism's dispatchEvent() method.

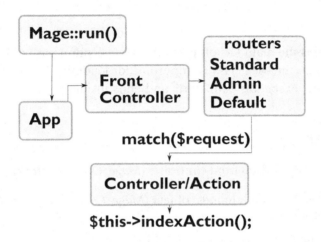

Figure 4.3

This directory listing shows all the files (except base Zend Framework files) that are involved in dispatching a request to the proper module. The directory layout has nothing to do with the class hierarchy, it is simply a product of class naming and PHP's autoloading capabilities.

```
Core
|- Controller/
|  |- Front/
|  |  |- Action.php
|  |  '- Router.php
|  |- Request/
|  |  '- Http.php
|  |- Response/
|  |  '- Http.php
|  '- Varien/
|     |- Action.php
|     |- Front.php
|     '- Router/
```

```
|          |- Abstract.php
|          |- Admin.php
|          |- Default.php
|          '- Standard.php
```

The App Model

The "App" model is the main kickoff point for the execution path of any request to Magento. Although the Mage class is important for loading all sorts of classes and configurations, the execution path starts and ends inside the *App*. The App is responsible for:

- Initializing the system cache

- Instantiating the default front controller (*Mage_Core_Controller_Varien_Front*)

- Instantiating the default request object (*Mage_Core_Controller_Request_Http*)

The Front Controller

From here, the responsibility transfers to the front controller. The front controller has an array of "*routers*" that it uses to decide which module the URL should trigger. This correlation between URL and module name is defined in the config.xml files. The available routers are:

- Standard

- Admin

- Default (only used for 404s)

The definition of a match between a router and a module looks like this for the Customer module:

```
<routers>
    <customer>
        <use>standard</use>
```

```
            <args>
                <module>Mage_Customer</module>
                <frontName>customer</frontName>
            </args>
        </customer>
    </routers>
```

Routers

Once a router has found a match of the first part of the URL to a defined **frontName** value from the XML, this value gets directly translated into a module name with a little adjustment to the capitalization of the words. The controller and the action names are taken from the URL as diagrammed above. If any value is missing, the defaults are taken from the core XML config via the getDefault method.

When specifying a URL, you don't always specify exactly which *module, controller*, and *action* you want to run. A request to example.com/customer/ does not fully specify which controller of the customer module, nor which action to run. If any indicators of module, controller, or action are missing from the URL the values are read from the default tag under web, then under front (default/web/front). By default, the CMS supplies these XML values it its own config.xml file. You can change these values in the administrative back-end under the menu items System > Configuration > Web. If the XML values happen to be completely missing, the fall-back values of core, index, and again, index are used for the values of module, controller, and action, respectively.

Actions

Actions are classes that extend Mage_Core_Controller_Front_Action which, in turn, extends Mage_Core_Controller_Varien_Action. Actions also have a dispatch method, but this method dispatches the request to an **action** method. Action methods have the word "Action" appended to their names to distinguish them from normal class methods. Appending a word to the method name also helps to stop people from running unexpected methods from the URL. Imagine someone requesting example.com/index.php/customer/account/__destruct. If the system did not protect action names, the resulting method call would look something like this:

```
$controllerInstance->__destruct();
```

Something like this could potentially be a vector to open up attacks on your site. But, I digress, Magento **does** protect the action method names by appending Action to any value taken from the URL, so this argument is purely academic.

During the dispatch event, the preDispatch method is called, and following the actual execution of the action method, the postDispatch method is called. By default, the postDispatch will save the current URL into the user's session as the last URL visited.

Action and action methods are where the primary business logic for a request happens. Typically the action methods will load a model or two based on IDs or other URL parameters, kick off a few methods of these models, and then run the layout sequence. Having the action methods be responsible for outputting their own layout is an important issue to understand. This makes it more difficult to integrate with other systems, as you cannot as easily supplant your own layout or templating methods after executing the business logic. Also, it does not allow for any "post dispatch" logic to make any alterations to the output.

Chapter 5

Database Design

Magento's database design is one of its most controversial aspects. Key data are modeled using the **Entity Attribute Value** method (EAV). Utilizing an EAV modeling pattern allows for unlimited attributes on any product, category, customer, or order, but EAV also depletes a programmer's ability to write ad-hoc queries against the data.

Before we delve deep into Magento's database design, we will look at the basic way of communicating with the database - the resource.

Resources and Database Connections

The role of a *resource* in Magento is to manage database connections. Resources are defined under the global XML tag of any config.xml file. To make a new database connection you would add XML like the following to any config.xml file. Each resource has a name of the form module/name and each connection has a name. Connection names are generally of the pattern module_read, module_write, or module_setup.

```
<resources>
  <default_setup>
    <connection>
      <host>localhost</host>
      <username></username>
      <password></password>
```

```
    <dbname>magento</dbname>
    <model>mysql4</model>
    <initStatements>SET NAMES utf8</initStatements>
    <type>pdo_mysql</type>
    <active>1</active>
  </connection>
</default_setup>
....
```

The format should be mostly self explanatory, most of these values end up being passed to the Zend_Db_Adapter_Abstract class. The initStatements tag is executed upon every connection to the database server. The model tag seems unnecessary, perhaps it was part of an idea that didn't pan-out completely. The type tag refers to one of two connection types defined in the global app/etc/config.xml file. Only pdo_mysql and mysqli are implemented at the moment.

To retrieve a Magento database connection we must first get a resource. If you require a generic database handle, you can use the name core/resource for the resource name, and core_write for the connection name. The Mage::getSingleton method keeps track of all classes loaded through it as singletons and returns a previously initialized object if the name matches. Each module may have its own database settings - usernames and passwords - or it might even be connecting to a separate database server, so be sure to use the most appropriate resource name when you can. In a default setup, all of Magento's connections use the settings of default_setup, default_write, or default_read.

```
$write = Mage::getSingleton('core/resource')
        ->getConnection('core_write');

if ($write instanceof Zend_Db_Adapter_Abstract) {
  echo get_class($write);
}
//outputs: Varien_Db_Adapter_Pdo_Mysql
```

Master Slave Setup

As you can see, the construction of database connections as named resources means that the system is ready for a "Master-Slave" database setup. You change the settings of the resource `default_write` to point to one MySQL database and all write operations will be sent to that database. You must be diligent in your own code to properly request `*_read` and `*_write` connections if you plan on setting up a master-slave situation.

The `default_setup` must be left to point to the slave databases as it is used to write information to upon module installation, and it is read from every request to verify that a module is up to date.

The `default_read` resource is not easily modifiable to read from a pool of MySQL slaves. One solution to this is to use a hostname value that is different for each frontend Web server with Magento installed. On Linux, this can be done easily by modifying the `/etc/hosts` file. But, this solution leads to a one-to-one mapping of Web servers to MySQL slaves, which is not always desirable. The problem of balancing read requests amongst all slave databases is not unique to Magento. Various other techniques exist to spread the load across slave databases evenly, but these solutions are beyond the scope of this book.

Models and Resource Models

All Magento *models* extend the base `Mage_Core_Model_Abstract` class. This class helps any model save itself to the database in a straight `property-to-column name` manner. The model, when saving, calls up its own resource singleton and passes **itself** (`$this`) to the resource's `save` method. The resource is then scripted to collect any values from the model's internal `_data` array and prepare an insert or an update statement with those values.

Model's have a `_getResource` method which retrieves a previously setup resource. This resource is initialized by the `init` method using a resource name of the pattern `module_name`. The *name* portion of that pattern represents the final portion of a class name. The prefix of the class name is specified by a portion of the XML in the module's `etc/config.xml`. If class names have the term `Mysql4` in their names, they are generally straight model resources. If the word `Entity` appears in the class name, then the resource is an EAV Entity.

Let's look at the *Wishlist* module as an example. In the `config.xml` of the wishlist module we see a `resourceModel` tag under the main definition of models. The value of this `resourceModel` tag points to another XML tag under the `models` tag. The `class` tag of this new definition specifies the class name prefix for any resource of this module. The following code shows how the sample XML file would produce a resource for the wishlist module.

```php
$wish = Mage::getResourceSingleton('wishlist/wishlist');
echo get_class($wish);
//outputs: Mage_Wishlist_Model_Mysql4_Wishlist
```

```xml
...
<global>
    <models>
        <wishlist>
            <class>Mage_Wishlist_Model</class>
            <resourceModel>wishlist_mysql4</resourceModel>
        </wishlist>
        <wishlist_mysql4>
            <class>Mage_Wishlist_Model_Mysql4</class>
            <entities>
                <wishlist>
                    <table>wishlist</table>
                </wishlist>
                <item>
                    <table>wishlist_item</table>
                </item>
            </entities>
        </wishlist_mysql4>
...
```

EAV Design

EAV can be thought of as "*vertical*" modeling instead of "*horizontal*" modeling of columns in a database table. Instead of a table consisting of a number of columns, denoting attributes of a conceptual piece of data, the attributes are stored in one column of a separate table. The differences between traditional table design and EAV table design of an example "user" table are shown below.

```
Traditional User Table
table: user
```

```
+---------------------------------------------------------+
| user_id | username | password | first_name | last_name |
+=========+==========+==========+-===========+===========+
|       1 |    steve |    [enc] |      Steve |     Smith |
+---------+----------+----------+------------+-----------+
|       2 |   ronnie |    [enc] |     Ronnie |     Smith |
+---------+----------+----------+------------+-----------+
```

This seemingly simple (and lacking) table would require at least 3 tables to capture the same data when using an EAV methodology.

EAV Style Tables

table: user_entity
```
+--------------------------------+
| user_id | username | password |
+=========+==========+==========+
|       1 |    steve |    [enc] |
+---------+----------+----------+
|       2 |   ronnie |    [enc] |
+---------+----------+----------+
```

table: user_varchar
```
+--------------------------------------+
| entity_id | attribute_id |    value |
+===========+==============+==========+
|         1 |            1 |    Steve |
+-----------+--------------+----------+
|         2 |            1 |   Ronnie |
+-----------+--------------+----------+
|         1 |            2 |    Smith |
+-----------+--------------+----------+
|         2 |            2 |    Smith |
+-----------+--------------+----------+
```

table: eav_attribute
```
+-------------------------------------------------------+
| attribute_id |       name | display |    type |
+==============+============+=========+=========+
|            1 | first_name |   First | varchar |
+--------------+------------+---------+---------+
|            2 |  last_name |    Last | varchar |
+--------------+------------+---------+---------+
```

As you can see from looking at the chart, adding a new attribute to a user simply involves adding a new record in the `eav_attribute` table. Adding a new attribute does not involve altering tables to add any new columns. This opens the door for graphical interfaces to easily manage adding new attributes to most parts of the system, while keeping the database schema consistent across installations.

Notice that the `eav_attribute` table has extra type information. In EAV systems, the key to having a flexible, workable system is meta-data **about** the attributes. Adding more columns to `eav_attribute` could allow for information about the attributes, like how attributes are grouped together, whether or not values are required, or if the attribute should be restricted to certain entity types (should you allow "first_name" for a product, or just a user?).

One downside to working with an EAV database is that the table design seems too loose. There is not one single source for the definition of a **user** that can easily be seen with traditional database tools and queries. Working with Magento's core data components is most easily done by utilizing the core libraries and their methods instead of directly running queries on the database. See the *Quick Answers* chapter for an example of a skeletal script to allow for writing quick database maintenance scripts.

EAV versus Normalization

Developers might wonder, "how is EAV different than normalization?" And the answer is, not much. Normalization, when it comes to abstracting attributes into one-to-many style tables is concerned with proper design from a database point of view. Not all one-to-many relationships are required in all situations. But, with the EAV style, all attributes are abstracted, or "normalized" into join tables, regardless if they violate traditional normalization rules.

The reason that attributes are put into join tables, regardless of traditional normalization rules, is because it is believed, by the application developers, that the running application will have too many unknown attributes to be properly designed for.

Entities

An *entity* is a core thing that is being modeled. In Magento, a product is modeled as an entity, but the product's SKU is not an entity, it is too simple. The difference can be likened to the difference between objects and object properties. *Objects* are *entities*, and *object properties* are *attributes*.

Entities extend Magento's **resource** objects and resources are simply connections to the database (actually they manage the different read/write connections and automatically figure out table names based on convention). Basically, *Entities* are "core" things that pair up to selected *Models* and help them save to the database. Entities behave mostly like resource models, as they are just a special sub-class of resources.

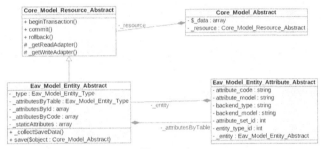

Figure 5.1

In the chart shown in Figure 5.1, we can see that a core *Model* has a *Resource*. This resource can be a plain resource, one which simply saves row data, or an *Entity*. Entities have a number of *Entity_Attributes*. References to these attributes are held in a number of attributes, allowing for quick reference look-up from a number of aspects: by table name, by id, or by attribute code.

Default Entities

By default, Magento comes with 26 entity types installed:

- catalog_category

- catalog_product

- creditmemo
- creditmemo_comment
- creditmemo_item
- customer
- customer_address
- invoice
- invoice_comment
- invoice_item
- invoice_payment
- order
- order_address
- order_item
- order_payment
- order_status_history
- quote
- quote_address
- quote_address_item
- quote_address_rate
- quote_item
- quote_payment
- shipment

- shipment_comment

- shipment_item

- shipment_track

Every entity listed (with the exception of credit memos, shipments, and invoices) has a corresponding "*entity*" table in the database. Credit memos, shipment tracking, and invoices are all saved in the same set of tables that orders are saved in.

Defining Entities

Resources and entities are highly correlated in the Magento codebase. All entities extend **resources** to gain access to database connections. This is a shame, since a lot of method names seem to use the two words "resource" and "entity" interchangeably.

```
...
<global>
    <models>
        <sales>
            <class>Mage_Sales_Model</class>
            <resourceModel>sales_entity</resourceModel>
        </sales>
        <sales_entity>
            <class>Mage_Sales_Model_Entity</class>
        </sales_entity>
...
</global>
...
```

As you can see from the above code, the `<resourceModel>` tag points to the "sales_entity" model name, which in-turn specifies a class name prefix of `Mage_Sales_Model_Entity`. The configuration for all modules does not follow this pattern.

Entities are entities, as explained above in the EAV section. But there are some database tables that **don't** use the EAV style; `poll`, `newsletter`, and `wishlist` are some of the very few tables that don't use the EAV pattern. For these modules, ones that don't use the EAV pattern, the resource models generally use the prefix *Resource* instead of *Entity*.

Saving Entities

An entity works with a model to save data to a number of different tables. The `_collectSaveData` works with the model and the entities' own collection of `Entity_Attributes` to gather the necessary information to save to the database. The `_collectSaveData` routine returns an associative array containing the keys: `newObject`, `entityRow`, `insert`, `update`, and `delete`. Each key represents a nested array of information which is processed by `_processSaveData`. The `_processSaveData` method makes multiple database calls, one for `entityRow` and one for each child of `insert`, `update`, or `delete`. The `newObject` key holds a reference to the model which will receive a new ID if the entity row data was successfully saved to the database.

Entity Attributes

Entity attributes work much like a regular property of an object, only they contain much more meta-data than a normal object property. If you are looking at the database table `eav_attribute` you'll see a column `attribute_code`. The attribute's `attribute_code` works as a key to the model's private `_data` array.

The entity attribute also specifies the table to which the data is saved. Normally, an entity attribute will use the table name of its parent entity and append its own type to the end. So an entity table of `customer` and an entity attribute of `firstname`, with a backend_type of `varchar` would result in storing the firstname value in `customer_entity_varchar`. This behavior can be overridden by specifically supplying a value for `backend_table` in the database for the definition of your entity attribute.

The number one thing to keep in mind when dealing with entity attributes is that they are merely instructions for **saving**, and **loading** attribute information. It is true that they are used for displaying information on the front-end, but most of your work creating Magento modules will probably have you debugging the database values more than debugging front-end display logic. I say to keep this in mind because the actual *values* of the attributes are stored on the entity object itself, in its private *_data* array. So, don't look to the attribute for a method like *getValue*. The proper way to render attribute values of an entity object is with the attribute's *frontend* renderer.

Attribute Values

A prime example of using the entity attributes for displaying data is in the catalog module's *product view* block. The *getAdditionalData* method cycles through a product's loaded attributes and stores the rendered value in an array, which the template then prints out. The *getFrontend* method of an attribute retrieves a special rendering object which understands how to display an attribute value. Some attributes, like Yes/No style attributes are stored in the database as ones and zeros, but is displayed in the catalog as either Yes or No. It is the job of the *frontend* object to render the value correctly.

```
$attributes = $product->getAttributes();
foreach ($attributes as $attribute) {
  if ($attribute->getIsVisibleOnFront()
      && $attribute->getIsUserDefined()) {

    $value = $attribute->getFrontend()->getValue($product);
    if (strlen($value) && $product->hasData(
        $attribute->getAttributeCode())) {

      $data[$attribute->getAttributeCode()] = array(
        'label' => $attribute->getFrontend()->getLabel(),
        'value' => $value
          )
      );
    }
  }
}
```

Notice how the product gets passed to *getValue*. The *frontend* object inspects the product for a value based on the attribute code with a call to *getData*, passing the attribute code as a parameter.

Collections

Working with *entities* allows you to load and save complex relationships to and from the database. But, most of the time when we think of database queries we want to write a SELECT statement that gives use a result with multiple rows. The entity models are not able to do that. Entities are designed to load one item, or *record*, at a time.

Only being able to deal with one record at a time means that we must know that records primary ID value to load it. But, what happens when we want to select all records from the database matching some criteria. Normally, a simple SELECT statement with a WHERE clause would work. But, things are not that simple when dealing with entities. Not all of the data that makes up an entity lives in one table, so we need to JOIN more tables. To properly construct a WHERE clause we would have to know exactly which tables our specific data is stored in. Even if we inspect the database and find the exact table, it's not guaranteed to stay the same after upgrading Magento to a new version. This is the problem that *collections* solve. Loading an arbitrary number of records based on criteria is the job of entity *collection*.

Collections come in two varieties - resource collections, and entity collections. Resource collections are just a stripped down version of the entity collections, so we won't cover them here.

Probably the most useful method of a collection is the *addAttributeToFilter* method. This method takes an attribute code and a condition.

```
$products = Mage::getModel('catalog/product')->getCollection();
$products->addAttributeToFilter('sku', '9999');
$products->load();
foreach($products as $_prod) {
    var_dump($_prod->getData());
}
```

In the above example, the condition is a simple string, but the condition can also be an array. When passing a condition array, the key of the array designates the type of comparison. The type can be eq, for equals, like for like comparisons, gt for a greater than comparison, or many one of more. The complete list can be found in the source code for the method _getConditionSql in the class Varien_Data_Collection_Db. Here is the same example above, but searching for an array of product IDs.

```
$products = Mage::getModel('catalog/product')->getCollection();
$products->addAttributeToFilter('entity_id',
        array('in'=> array(1,2,36,35) )
);
$products->load();
foreach($products as $_prod) {
```

```
    var_dump($_prod->getData());
}
//runs the query:
/*
SELECT 'e'.* FROM 'catalog_product_entity' AS 'e'
WHERE (e.entity_type_id = '4') AND (e.entity_id in (1, 2, 36, 35))
*/
```

If you wish to see the query being run, you can pass *true* to the collection's load method. This will print the exact query being run against the database.

The preceding examples result in some pretty basic SQL. If we want to grab complex results, like loading all the entity's attribute values, we can use the addAttributeToSelect method. For reporting purposes, you will most likely just want to add all attribute values to your query, so we will pass the wildcard * to this method.

```
$products = Mage::getModel('catalog/product')->getCollection();
$products->addAttributeToFilter('entity_id',
        array('in'=> array(1,2,36,35) )
);
$products->addAttributeToSelect('*');
$products->load();
foreach($products as $_prod) {
   var_dump($_prod->getData());
}
```

You will notice that a lot more data is printed in this version, after we have added all attributes to the select statement. The collections classes use the Zend Framework database classes under the hood to construct all the necessary queries to pull data out of the database. For more information on the Zend Framework database libraries, look at the source code in lib/Zend/Db/ or visit http://framework.zend.com.

This is only scratching the surface of the SQL that you can generate with collections. Look at the Eav/Model/Entity/Collection/Abstract.php file for a full list of methods to manipulate your SQL. Remember that collections are the only way to load entity objects if you need to use a WHERE clause other than querying against the table's primary key field. When dealing with non-entity models, you can always write raw SQL and run it against a resource connection. Technically, you *can* write raw SQL to load entities and all of their associated attribute values, but you might want to try using Magento's built-in query methods first.

Chapter 6

Custom Modules

In this chapter we are going to discover how to create a custom module. To start out, we will make some simple modifications to the *product view* page.

The Filesystem

You might have noticed that all of Magento's modules are located under a directory called Mage, short for *Magento*. This directory, which is located under app/code/core, can be thought of as the entire Magento application. But, you can also think of the Mage directory as just a namespace, lending another prefixed name to every piece of code that falls under it.

In fact, this directory has no other function than to simply add naming consistency to all the classes under it, it has no bearing on the inclusion of modules into the "Magento" application. Keeping this fact in mind we can initiate a directory structure for our own module, using our company's or organization's name where we would normally see "Mage".

```
app/code/core/
          Mage/
                Admin/
                Catalog/
                Cms/
```

```
local/
      Company/
            NewProduct/
```

In the above directory layout we can see a new module called "NewProduct" under the `Company` directory under `app/code/local/`. Using our own organization's name keeps our modules from conflicting with any other installable user contributions. If, for example, another developer decides to make a module called "NewProduct" just like our module, but it has different features, we can safely install both if we keep the top level prefixes different.

The Shell Module

You will probably be creating at least a few Magento modules. If this is the case, it is very beneficial to be familiar with starting new modules. All modules covered in this book are meant to be installed under `app/code/local`. This is referred to as the "local code pool". We will create all modules under a parent directory called `Company`, you can treat this as a package name. This will help to distinguish our modules – ones that we develop for our company or ourselves – from the core Magento modules, which are all under the package `Mage`.

Default Directories

Whenever this book tells you to initialize a new module you should create a directory structure like the following under `app/code/local`:

```
|- Company/
|   - ModuleName/
|      |- Block/
|      |- controllers/    <-- lower case, plural
|      |- Model/
|      |- Helper/
|      |- etc/
|      |   - config.xml  <-- shell XML file
|        - sql/
```

This will ensure that we have all the necessary directories to create the most common parts of any module.

There are two parts of a module that cannot be defined within a module's own directory. One part of a module that is not self-contained is the design portion. The templates and layout settings for a module live in a separate directory, the app/design folder. To counteract this, you can create a design directory with sub-directories of layout and templates. Dealing with the skin directory can be tackled the same way as the design directory. Magento's skin directory is for storing CSS files and images or icons.

The other portion of a module that needs to exist but which is not kept under a module's own directory is an XML file which instructs Magento to turn-on your module.. Under the directory app/etc/modules there exist a number of XML files which tell the system which modules are on or off. These files are generally grouped by the package, or company name, and each file can enable or disable multiple modules. Without this, your module will not be activated and no configuration settings will be read. You can include the necessary XML file to activate your module inside the module's directory, but you need to copy this file to app/etc/modules to complete the installation.

Default Files

Almost every custom Magento module is going to need the same basic settings as any other module. As a result, a basic config.xml will serve our needs quite well. Put the following code into etc/config.xml.

```xml
<?xml version="1.0"?>
<config>
    <!-- turn on our module, required for install support -->
    <modules>
        <Company_ModuleName>
            <version>0.1.0</version>
        </Company_ModuleName>
    </modules>

    <global>
        <!-- turn on models -->
        <models>
            <modulename>
```

```
                    <class>Company_ModuleName_Model</class>
                </modulename>
            </models>
            <!-- turn on models -->
            <blocks>
                <modulename>
                    <class>Company_ModuleName_Model</class>
                </modulename>
            </blocks>

            <!-- turn on database connections -->
            <resources>
                <!-- setup is needed for automatic installation -->
                <modulename_setup>
                        <use>default_setup</use>
                </modulename_setup>
                <modulename_write>
                        <use>default_write</use>
                </modulename_write>
                <modulename_read>
                        <use>default_read</use>
                </modulename_read>
            </resources>
        </global>
    </config>
```

This XML file will give us the absolute basics for a working model. Don't worry about turning on models or blocks even if we don't need them. The XML tags don't actively change anything, they simply live in the global XML configuration DOM.

The last XML file we need is the one that turns our module on. Not all directories are treated as modules and scanned for *config* files, a module must be specified in the global directory app/etc/modules. Place this XML into a file in app/etc/modules and call it Company_Module.xml.

```
<?xml version="1.0"?>
<config>
    <modules>
        <Company_ModuleName>
            <active>true</active>
            <codePool>local</codePool>
        </Company_ModuleName>
    </modules>
</config>
```

Module Requirements

Let's take a moment to read over and understand the requirements of our new module. These requirements are contrived to provide the best demonstration of how to create a custom module and might not make sense for all e-stores.

- Must force certain products to be ordered in specified quantity intervals (12, 24, 36, etc.)

- Must limit maximum allowable quantity ordered to 24 cases for certain products

These two simple requirements allow us to focus on understanding Magento modules while adding real value to the system and avoiding unnecessarily complicated (at this point) SQL.

Plan of Attack

Here is an overview of the steps we will perform to make the first requirement of this new module a reality:

- Create a shell module

- Activate the module with a `config.xml` file

- Create the desired effect in a template file

- Connect the template to a template *block*

- Conditionally turn the new feature on and off

Configuration Files

Magento does not recognize your module as being a module simply because you have created the directory in the proper place. An XML configuration needs to be put in the proper place detailing the existence of your module. Under the top level `app/etc/modules/` directory all XML files are scanned and the relevant modules are activated. Listing a module as **active** means that that module's own etc/config.xml file will also be scanned. So, the only information we need to place in the top level app/etc/modules/ folder is just enough information to turn our module on.

Below is the complete syntax of the XML file you need to activate your module. Save this XML in a file under app/etc/modules/Company_All.xml The syntax should be self-explanatory. Once this file is in place, you should be able to see your new module listed in the admin system configuration panel. Browse to *System > Configuration > Advanced* and you should see *Company_NewProduct* as an option to enable or disable. If you do not see your new module listed after creating the new XML file, ensure that Magento's caching is off (*System > Cache Management > All Cache: disable*) and remove any files in var/cache/.

```xml
<?xml version="1.0"?>
<config>
    <modules>
        <Company_NewProduct>
            <active>true</active>
            <codePool>local</codePool>
        </Company_NewProduct>
    </modules>
</config>
```

Config.xml

Once you have activated your new module, the system will scan your module's etc folder for any of the following XML files:

- config.xml (defines models, resources, and other settings for basic functionality)

- system.xml (defines admin menus and default settings for forms)

- convert.xml (works with the Dataflow component for importing / exporting data)

- install.xml (only used for one-time Magento installation)

The config.xml file is the chief file you will be using for setting up the configuration of your module. None of the other files are required. The XML files are not examined with respect to any module, so you will see most settings wrapped in tags that refer to the current module; tags like <Company_NewProduct>. Let's start with a simple config.xml and review what each part of the XML does.

```xml
<config>
    <modules>
        <Company_NewProduct>
            <version>0.7.32</version>
            <depends>
            <!-- no dependencies -->
            </depends>
        </Company_NewProduct>
    </modules>
    <global>
        <models></models>
        <resources></resources>
        <blocks></blocks>
        <newproduct><!-- config values --></newproduct>
    </global>
    <adminhtml>
        <menu></menu>
        <acl></acl>
        <events></events>
        <translate></translate>
    </adminhtml>
    <frontend>
        <routers></routers>
        <events></events>
        <translate></translate>
        <layout></layout>
    </frontend>
    <default>
        <config_vars><!-- config values --></config_vars>
    </default>
</config>
```

Modules Tag

The modules tag provides a way to define some basic information about your module. The version number is critical to automatic installation and upgrades. Without a version number none of the installation files under sql/module_setup will be run automatically. You can define dependencies for your module. Setting dependencies ensures that your module is included after the declared modules. This keeps your classes from breaking if they extend classes from another module. The modules tag is the same place to define your application as enabled or disabled and to specify in which *codePool* it lives. Since, your module is not scanned, and thus your module's config.xml isn't scanned, unless it is already enabled, we must specify the enabled status and the codePool in the app/etc/modules/ directory. Every XML file in app/etc/modules/ is always scanned.

Global Tag

The global tag is where you specify models, resources, blocks, and other configuration directives like entity definitions. The global block is always included on each request.

Adminhtml Tag

The adminhtml tag contains special settings which are only used by the back-end administration page. This tag is mostly used to define any special menus and access control you want specifically for the administrative back-end.

Frontend Tag

This tag is a lot like the adminhtml tag, except the values under it are strictly used on the front-end of Magento. This is where you can specify a custom *layout* XML file for your module. The *routers* tag lets you decide which of Magento's routers should trigger connections to your module.

Default Tag

The default tag allows you to specify any set of config variables needed for your module. The values are normally obtained with *getStoreConfig*, passing the name of your XML tags as a slash separated string. For better organization of these ad-hoc variables it is customary to wrap all of your settings in a tag that matches your module's name. The values in the default tag can be overwritten on the configuration page of the administrative back-end. Any changes to the defaults are inserted into the database table `core_config_data`. These modified values are still retrieved with a call to *getStoreConfig*.

Template Changes

Unfortunately, the module structure in Magento lacks the ability to include any sort of files containing design changes with the other files your module. All the template and layout files are kept in a directory completely separate from the business logic code. Keeping your custom template files and layout changes with your module is a good idea for developing and distributing your module. The only steps that would need to be taken are simply copying some files from one directory to another. In fact, this sort of post-installation procedures might be handled at the end of your installer script, but this idea is not duplicated anywhere else in Magento.

For now, we will create a `design` directory under your module with `template` and `layout` directories to match the directory app/design/frontend/default/default/.

```
local/
- Company/
   - NewProduct/
      |- etc/
      |  - config.xml
      - design/
         |- template/  <-- keep local template files here
          - layout/    <-- keep local layout files here
```

Our first step in creating this custom module is to simply make the HTML changes necessary to show the quantity input box as a **drop-down list**. This will force the user to make a quantity choice of only the displayed choices. Later, we will enhance the module by adding more features and configuration to this simple change.

In Figure 6.1, you can see three sections annotated with text balloons which show the XML syntax used to initiate that block. The entire *content* area of the page is rendered with the template catalog/product/view.phtml. Various sub-components of the page are called from within that template as $this->getChildHtml('blockName'). The sub-component areas must be defined in the layout XML as block tags nested

Figure 6.1

under the definition of the containing block (or under a reference tag if the block was defined elsewhere). The area that contains the quantity input box is part of the product_type_data block (when referring to block names, the *as* XML attribute overrides the *name* attribute). Let's start the templates for the custom module by copying the existing product_type_data template file to our own directory.

```
Starting from: app/design/frontend/default/default/

template/
|- catalog/
|   - product/
|     - view/
|       - type/
|         - simple.phtml  <-- copy this file...
|
  - newproduct/
    - product_view_type_simple.phtmltml  <-- ... as this file.
```

As you can see, we are "flattening" the file name from a complex, nested set of sub-directories to a more simplified view. Since our module will only have a limited number of template files, keeping them all in one directory should not pose a problem. The nesting of template files as Magento's default nesting is needlessly complex and provides no inherent benefit. Placing a file in the directory catalog/product/view/type/ and giving it a prefix of catalog_product_view_type has little to no impact throughout most of the system.

Now we can modify this template to include the HTML changes that are required for our "sell-by-case" feature. For now, we will simply write the hard-coded HTML to show a **drop-down** list and revise the file later to read values from a new block file. Modify your file by commenting out the initial quantity input box so that it looks like the example below.

```php
<?php if($_product->isSaleable()): ?>
    <fieldset class="add-to-cart-box">
        <legend><?php echo $this->__('Add Items to Cart') ?></legend>
        <span class="qty-box">
            <label for="qty"><?php echo $this->__('Qty') ?>:</label>
<!-- our custom changes -->
            <select name="qty" class="input-text" id="qty">
                <option value="12">12</option>
                <option value="24">24</option>
                <option value="36">36</option>
                <option value="48">48</option>
                <option value="60">60</option>
            </select>
<!--
        old input box
        <input name="qty" type="text" class="input-text qty"
            id="qty" maxlength="12" value="
            <?php echo $this->getMinimalQty($_product) ?>
            "/> -->
        </span>
```

Layout Changes

To view your changes, we must activate this new template in the layout system. Remember that the layout system is controlled by a number of XML files. The exact file that you would want to change depends on the module being used for any particular Web "hit". Viewing a product is considered to be part of the *catalog* module. Normally, the tag you want to search for in the XML is directly related to the URL. Unfortunately, the SEO URLs don't allow us to see the traditional URL that would map directly to a module-controller-action combination. Luckily, we have this book that lets us in on all the secrets of Magento, so we are aware that the page that shows us product info relates to the layout XML tag of `<catalog_product_view>`.

This particular layout change is not normal. When dealing with products, the different product *types* are now handled by special layout tags, called *layout update handles*. Special layout update handles are called by the controller file (usually) and are not specifically documented anywhere in the system. For now, though, we will just update the one layout handle for `PRODUCT_TYPE_simple` and activate our new template file. The changes to `catalog.xml` should look similar to the code below.

```
<!--
Additional block dependent on product type
-->
  <PRODUCT_TYPE_simple>
      <reference name="product.info">
          <!--
          <block type="catalog/product_view_type_simple"
            name="product.info.simple"
            as="product_type_data"
            template="catalog/product/view/type/simple.phtml"/>
          -->
          <block type="catalog/product_view_type_simple"
            name="product.info.simple"
            as="product_type_data"
            template="newproduct/product_view_type_simple.phtml"/>
      </reference>
  </PRODUCT_TYPE_simple>
```

Now you should be able to refresh any product info page and see a drop-down list of choices for quantity instead of the usual input box. If you do not see your changes, make sure that you have disabled caching in the backend administration area (*System > Cache Management*). If you still don't see your changes, try debugging the original `simple.phtml` file by putting syntax errors inside and refreshing the page, you should see a partial rendering of the page. If you still don't see your changes, try checking all the file names and the capitalization of all the names.

Overridding a Block

Now that the first step is done, we can start to make our feature more functional, by adding our own custom template block. Blocks act as the communication gateway for template files into the rest of the system. As it stands now, the quantity drop-down feature affects every single product in the system, and it only shows the quantity options that we have hardcoded into the HTML. The idea behind this feature is that some products are only sold by the case, and others are not, but that customers comparison shop for the item based on individual prices, not prices by the dozen. Using a block will help us inject some display logic "brains" into this feature.

Create a new class called ProductViewCase.php in a new Block directory under your NewProduct module. The class definition is below:

```php
<?php
/**
 * This class allows the template to check for a case count
 * variable.
 */
class Company_NewProduct_Block_ProductViewCase
    extends Mage_Catalog_Block_Product_View_Type_Simple {

    //getCaseCount()
    //hasCaseCount()
    //getMaxQty()
}
```

Here again, in this code sample, we have shortened the directory nesting level just for simplicity's sake by combining the last few words into ProductViewCase. Even with this code as simply a shell of logic we should be able to activate it, override the existing block, and see no errors on the product information screen. To do that, we must use the original block name as an XML tag name in our module's etc/config.xml file.

```xml
<?xml version="1.0"?>
<config>
  <modules>
      <Company_NewProduct>
      </Company_NewProduct>
  </modules>
<!-- add this block section to your config.xml -->
```

```
    <blocks>
        <catalog>
            <rewrite>
                <product_view_type_simple>
                    Company_NewProduct_Block_ProductViewCase
                </product_view_type_simple>
            </rewrite>
        </catalog>
    </blocks>
<!-- DONE: add this block section to your config.xml -->
</config>
```

Warning

Because of a bug in Magento's code that treats XML whitespace as significant, the contents of the above tag product_view_type_simple must be on one line. It is broken up only to fit on the page properly. If you were to were to use this XML exactly as written the code would try to instantiate a new object with a class name of with newline and space characters at the beginning and end.

Since the original block is of type catalog/product_view_type_simple, we must use the **catalog** tag to enclose any of our changes. The **rewrite** tag is used, specifically, to express the desire to override some class names with new ones. Normally, all blocks are defined as having a module-wide class prefix, as in the following XML taken from Catalog/etc/config.xml:

```
    <blocks>
        <catalog><class>Mage_Catalog_Block</class></catalog>
    </blocks>
```

This means, that for every block labeled catalog/product_view, the system will look for Mage_Catalog_Block_**Product_View** as the class name.

Now we will fill out our three methods of the block class.

```
class Company_NewProduct_Block_ProductViewCase
    extends Mage_Catalog_Block_Product_View_Type_Simple {

    /**
```

```
 * Return the value of "case_count" or 0
 *
 * return int quantity of product per case
 */
function getCaseCount() {
    $product = $this->getProduct();
    return intval($product->getCaseCount());
}


/**
 * Return true if this product is sold "by-the-case".
 *
 * return boolean
 */
function hasCaseCount() {
    $product = $this->getProduct();
    return $product->getCaseCount() > 1 ;
}

/**
 * Use Magento's stock level classes to determine the
 * maximum allowable quantity per order.
 *
 * return int
 */
function getMaximumQty() {
    $product = $this->getProduct();
    $stock = $product->getStockItem();
    return $stock->getMaxSaleQty();
}
}
```

In order for these methods to work properly, we need to add a variable called case_count to each product that we would like to sell by the case. Notice how $product->**getCaseCount()** automatically searches for an attribute with the code case_count. You will not find any method defined called getCaseCount() as this relies on PHP's magic method __call() to hunt down the proper properties of any object that extends Varien_Object.

Once these methods are complete, we need to modify our existing template to make use of them.

```
<span class="qty-box"><label for="qty">
```

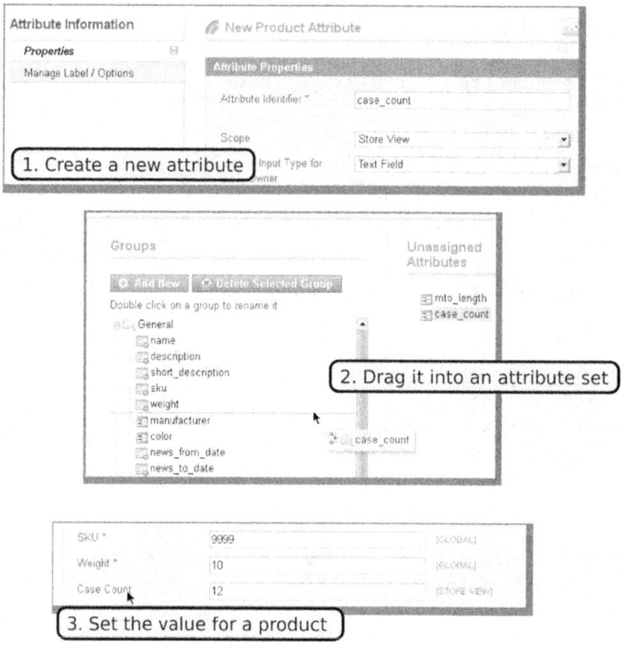

Figure 6.2

```php
<?php echo $this->__('Qty') ?>:</label>
<?php if ($this->hasCaseCount()): ?>
    <select name="qty" class="input-text" id="qty">
    <?php
        $caseCount = $this->getCaseCount();
        for( $x = $caseCount; $x <= $this->getMaximumQty();
            $x += $caseCount): ?>
        <option value="<?=$x;?>"><?=$x;?></option>
    <?php
        endfor;
    ?>
    </select>
<?php
    else:
?>
    <input name="qty" type="text" class="input-text qty"
      id="qty" maxlength="12"
      value="<?php echo $this->getMinimalQty($_product) ?>"/>
<?php
```

```
    endif;
?>
</span>
```

Conclusion

In this chapter you have seen how to make a module by collecting a few changes from other classes together under one roof. This technique should be used for any change that you want to make to Magento's core code classes. If you discover that you need to alter the behavior of files in `lib/` you can simply copy them to `app/code/local/` since the `include_path` is set to look there before the `lib` directory. For more advanced customization you will need to learn about event listeners, models and entities, and Magento's database design.

Chapter 7

CMS Integration

CMS Integration means different things to different people. Even the term CMS (Content Management System) has some variance in its definition. At the core of the integration feature is a desire to reuse a user's login credentials and share a single sign-on process between two software packages. Some organizations have an existing community with a large list of registered users. Some organizations do not have an existing CMS, or they want to leverage a new CMS to increase search engine rankings.

For existing CMS, the store is generally an add-on feature where existing users can purchase merchandise related to the content. We will call this type of setup the "CMS-driven" integration. Organizations that are looking to republish product content to new or existing blogs, forums, wikis or "static" pages we will refer to that integration style as "store-driven" integration.

CMS Driven Approach

Anecdotally, I would say the most asked for integration is with Joomla/Mambo or Drupal CMS systems. This would fall under the "CMS-driven" scenario where people are looking to Magento to fulfill a secondary need to sell merchandise while leveraging the existing user base.

At a bare minimum, user integration consists of re-using a user's login name and password to allow for signing in to either site without any extra work from the user.

This can be accomplished with a simple export of login information from one system and importing it into the other. If we do this, we are left with two separate databases full of user information.

Technical Considerations

What happens when a user wants to change their password? Well, it depends on where they do it. If they change their password in Magento, then the two systems will have different values. We could rectify this with scheduled synchronization routines between the two databases, but when two records are different we have to ask ourselves, which is the correct one? Without a *timestamp* for each value change we don't know if the user changed their password in the CMS database or in Magento's, all we know is that the two values are different. This situation is called the "Non-Authoritative Data Source" syndrome, or *NADS*.

To avoid NADS, we will only use one database as the source for all login information. In addition to creating confusion, importing and exporting the data between Magento and another CMS might be technically impossible if the database password hashing schemes are different.

Even though we have made a decision about how to integrate the login information, it does not tackle the **single sign-on** issue (SSO). A user would still have to login to either the CMS, to post comments or contribute content, and then also login to Magento to make purchases. To allow the user an SSO experience we need to share session information between the two systems, or, at least, initiate two different sessions at the same time.

We will take the approach of initiating sessions on both systems whenever a user logs-in to either one. This will not allow us to directly share session information between the two sites, but this need is low because of the specialized nature of data stored in a session for a particular piece of software. To think about it another way ask yourself, "What would Magento do with the last 5 forum topics that a user visited?" or "What would Joomla do with the last 2 products that I viewed?". When looked at it that way, you can see how specialized the data is for each system. I'm not saying that cross-pollinating the information is never valuable, I'm saying that for the majority of integration scenarios that it is a *want* not a *need*.

The UserConnect Module

To accomplish our goals of sharing login information and starting dual sessions between a CMS and Magento we will start a new module called UserConnect. Refer to the *Custom Modules* chapter for how to initialize a new shell module.

Database Design

Magento's EAV database makes using any other table of users a challenge. We must remember that Magento treats customers as *entities*. Anything related to the customer is an entity_attribute; this includes the password hash, the ID of the user's default shipping and billing addresses, and the user's first and last names. So, a typical, flat database table for users might look like this:

```
+----------------------------------------------------------------+
| user_id | username | password | first_name | last_name | ship_id |
+=========+==========+==========+-===========+===========+========+
|       1 |    steve |    [enc] |      Steve |     Smith |     1 |
+---------+----------+----------+------------+-----------+-------+
|       2 |   ronnie |    [enc] |     Ronnie |     Smith |     2 |
+---------+----------+----------+------------+-----------+-------+
```

Magento's tables are organized according to EAV methodology. It would require multiple pages to list exactly how Magento stores the same user information as the above table shows. But, we can summarize the data relationships in a graph like the one in Figure 7.1.

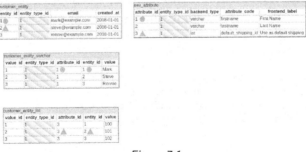

Figure 7.1

As you can see, storing the same information in Magento requires four tables. The shaded columns highlight the entity_type_id field. This value will be the same for all entities of the same type. For example, all *customers* have an entity_type_id of **1**. Therefore, any attribute that could relate to a customer, such as their default shipping id, also has an entity_type_id of **1**.

In the graph above, the circles represent related data for the notion of "User 1's firstname". The triangles represent the relationship of the datum "User 2's default shipping address id". Note how the backend_type column dictates to which table we must relate to get the value of the attribute.

You might think the entity_type_id field is redundant, and it could be considered such, but see the *Database* chapter for an explanation of why it is useful.

Creating New Entities

In your UserConnect module we will create a new entity to handle the loading and saving of the user object to and from a database. Creating the entity the easy part. The hard part is trying to keep some of the attributes from the customer entity not to follow us along to our new (read: already existing) database. What I mean by this is that we do **not** want to store all attributes about a user in our CMS database. Perhaps our CMS does not handle shipping addresses, so we probably don't have a place for storing the default shipping address ID anywhere in our system. Forcing Magento to split up the entity and the entity's attributes is the most involved part of this module.

Let's start by adding some XML to our config.xml to turn on entities for our module. Hopefully you already have the *models* portion of your config filled out according to the shell module in the *Custom Modules* chapter. We need to add one resourceModel tag under the models tag where we specify our class prefix for models.

```
...
  <models>
    <userconnect>
        <class>Company_UserConnect_Model</class>
        <resourceModel>userconnect_entity</resourceModel>
    </userconnect>
  ..
```

The `resourceModel` tag instructs Magento to look in another spot for more detailed information about any *resource models* that our module might use. For this example, we will reference `userconnect_entity` as the tag that holds more resource model information.

Using `_entity` is simply convention to distinguish EAV entities from regular resource models. The following XML goes under the `models` tag outside of our `userconnect` tag.

```
...
  <models>
...
    <userconnect_entity>
        <class>Company_UserConnect_Model_Entity</class>
        <entities>
            <customer_entity>
                <table>user</table>
            </customer_entity>
        </entities>
    </userconnect_entity>
```

Models

When overriding existing entities, the only way to get them to play with the *models* to which they are associated is to override the core model as well. The model's `init` method sets which resource model the regular model uses. So, we must add some more XML to our `config.xml` so that we can override the core `Customer` class model.

```
...
  <models>
...
  <customer>
    <rewrite>
      <customer>Company_UserConnect_Model_Customer</customer>
    </rewrite>
  </customer>
```

When we copy the customer class model over to our `Model` directory, we want to change the class name to match ours, and change the *extends* to the original class.

We only want to change a few things in the customer model, and the rest of the methods can fall back to the way the parent model behaves.

Below is a list of all the methods that we want to keep in our sub-class, the rest can be deleted.

```
Company_UserConnect_Model_Customer
 extends Mage_Customer_Model_Customer
{
 function _construct()
 public function authenticate($login, $password)
 public function loadByEmail($customerEmail)
 protected function _beforeSave()
 public function changePassword($newPassword, $checkCurrent=true)
 public function setPassword($password)
 public function hashPassword($password, $salt=null)
 public function generatePassword($length=6)
 public function validatePassword($password)
 public function encryptPassword($password)
 public function decryptPassword($password)
```

Entities

Now, we get to create new entities. Let's start by copying the default customer entity. If you've been poking around in the `Customer/etc/config.xml` you probably already know which file it is. Copy `Customer/Model/Entity/Customer.php` to our own `UserConnect/Model/Entity/` directory. Create the `Entity` directory if you haven't already.

For this class, we will **not** extend the original. If we forget to override or customize a particular part of our entity we do **not** want the default behavior of the customer entity. This would send data to two different locations simultaneously. But we still want our class to behave like an entity, so we need to extend `Mage_Eav_Model_Entity_Abstract`.

First, we will change the constructor. We will be using our own connections, see the *Custom Modules* chapter for defining your own database connections. The code sample below shows what your constructor should look like.

```
class Company_UserConnect_Model_Entity_Customer
```

```
extends Mage_Eav_Model_Entity_Abstract {

public function __construct() {
    $this->setType('userconnect');

    $resource = Mage::getSingleton('core/resource');
    $this->setConnection(
        $resource->getConnection('userconnect_read'),
        $resource->getConnection('userconnect_write')
    );
}
}
```

Entities in the Database

The constructor's first order of business is to set this entity's type with setType. The type is a code that matches up to an entity_type_code in the database in the table eav_entity_type. The eav_entity_type table has lots of configuration points for your entity. The field entity_model allows you to specify which entity model class file you want to use. The format of this field is *module/resourcemodelcode*. The resourcemodelcode portion represents a class name, but it also gets a class prefix attached to the front. The prefix is the value of the class tag which is *under* the value of your resourceModel tag. Here's an example:

```
...
  <models>
      <userconnect>
          <class>Company_UserConnect_Model</class>
          <resourceModel>userconnect_entity</resourceModel>
      </userconnect>
      <userconnect_entity>
          <class>Company_UserConnect_Model_Entity</class>
  <!-- a model_entity value in the database of
      "userconnect/customer"
      would result in a classname of
      Company_UserConnect_Model_Entity_Customer
  -->
```

The next thing the constructor does is set the default read and write connections. You will want to setup your own connections for this module so that you can talk to a different database. See the *Magento Modules* chapter for the XML to create your own database connections.

To insert our own entity type, normally we would use a setup resource model and call its `installEntities` method. But, it doesn't allow us to completely control all of the values of the `eav_entity_type` table. So we will use some raw SQL. This is a good candidate for putting into the `sql` directory for automatic installation.

```
    INSERT INTO 'eav_entity_type' (
'entity_type_code',
'attribute_model',
'entity_model',
'entity_table',
'value_table_prefix',
'entity_id_field')
    VALUES (
'userconnect',
'',
'userconnect/customer',
'userconnect/customer_entity',
'customer_entity',
'user_id'
);
```

Configuring the Entity

If you were to try to login right now, you'd see some error about a missing `website_id`. This is because our CMS's database tables do not have a `website_id` field (hopefully). Now we enter the process of configuring the entity, which can largely be done by trial and error. Change the `_getDefaultEntities()` method to return an empty array. Next, remove all references to `getSharingConfig` and `website_id` from the following methods:

- _beforeSave()

- _getLoadRowSelect()

- loadByEmail()

Passwords

Before we can login to Magento with our CMS logins, we need to adjust the customer model so that it processes passwords just like our other system. For this example, I assume that only the MD5 encrypted versions of passwords are stored in the CMS database.

Magento is able to decrypt its saved passwords. This can cause some problems for us if we have a database full of one-way hashed passwords, such as ones encrypted with MD5. One thing we can do is to create our own getPasswordHash method to return the regular password, which is already encrypted, so the customer model doesn't double the encryption.

```
public function getPasswordHash()
{
    return $this->getPassword();
}
```

Now, we only have two other password related changes and we will be done. The validatePassword method uses a core helper to centralize support for old and new Magento hashing schemes. But, to keep this example short, we won't override the helper, we will simply write our own validation routine. The last change is simply to change the hashPassword method to use a simple md5 call.

```
public function hashPassword($password, $salt=null)
{
    return md5(sha1($password));
}

public function validatePassword($password)
{
    if (!($hash = $this->getPasswordHash())) {
        return false;
    }
    return $this->hashPassword($password) === $hash;
}
```

You should now be able to login to Magento using a username and password from your CMS database.

Entity Attributes

You may have noticed that after you login, your user's first name and last name are missing. If they are not missing, then that means your CMS table that holds the login information also has *firstname* and *lastname* columns. First names and last names are most likely part of your existing CMS database. If they are not in the same table as the username, we'll cover how to get that data into Magento.

For other attributes, like the ID of the user's default shipping address, we will simply keep storing them in the existing Magento tables.

Creating Entity Attributes

In order for Magento to understand where we want to store our attribute values, we have to create new records in the table eav_attribute. This is akin to overriding code, but we must do it in the database by adding new records. We will create 2 new records, one for the default shipping address and one for the default billing address.

```
INSERT INTO 'eav_attribute' (
'entity_type_id',
'attribute_code',
'backend_model',
'backend_table',
'backend_type')
   VALUES (
'get this value from the userconnect
entity we made in the previous section',
'default_shipping',
'customer_entity_int',
'customer/customer_attribute_backend_billing',
'int'
);
```

Repeat this SQL and swap billing for shipping.

First and Last Names

The _getLoadRowSelect method constructs a Varien_Db_Select object (which extends the Zend_Db_Select object) which is responsible for loading up all of the core data for an entity. The values for any entity attributes that are part of this entity are loaded from the _getLoadAttributesSelect.

This is different from the loadAllAttributes method, which simply loads the meta-data about an attribute, but not values for any particular attribute of an object.

If we have a database where the firstname and lastname values are stored in another table, we can join that table to the main entity select.

Assume that we have an account table, with a foreign key called user_id which matches up to the primary key in our user table.

```
protected function _getLoadRowSelect($object, $rowId)
{
    //override this to rid where clause of ambiguity
    $select = $this->_read->select()
        ->from($this->getEntityTable())
        ->where($this->getEntityTable().'.'.
            $this->getEntityIdField()."=?", $rowId);

    $select->join('account', 'account.user_id=user.user_id','*');
    return $select;
}
```

We are specifying the entity's table in the "where" clause to remove ambiguity in the resulting SQL statement. If we didn't prepend the table, then the database would not know which user_id field we were referring to, since both the account table and the user table both have a user_id field.

Everything from the resulting query is stored on the object's private _data array. The object is, of course, our regular customer model. Remember this about Magento: you do not need special EAV attribute objects to load the attribute values of a model. You only need the EAV attribute objects to find out where the attribute value is living in the database and how to display it.

Dealing with Legacy Attributes

As of right now, there are a number of attributes of the customer entity that cannot be saved. When saved, the system attempts to save them into your CMS database under the same table names that Magento uses (i.e. customer_entity_int). This is a list of all the attributes of a customer. The email attribute isn't really used, it's stored directly in the customer_entity table. The first and last names don't need special handing, since they're already saved in our CMS table. The remainder, however, are still pretty important to Magento's operation. But they are not important at all to our CMS's functionality. So, we will shove them back into Magento by overriding key methods in our customer entity class, and revert the behavior back to normal Magento mode.

- created_in

- default_billing

- default_shipping

- email

- firstname

- group_id

- lastname

- password_hash

- store_id

- website_id

Update and Save Attributes

The saveAttribute and _updateAttribute methods need to be corrected. The default behavior is to use the same database connection as the parent entity, and this is not what we want. The fix is pretty easy. Copy the function definitions from Mage/Eav/Model/Entity/Abstract.php. What we're going to do is save our current database connection, swap in the old customer connection, call the parent method, then put our saved connection back in place.

```
//force attributes back into M
protected function _updateAttribute($object, $attribute,
                      $valueId, $value)
{
  $cmsWrite = $this->_write;
  $cmsRead = $this->_read;
  $cmsEntityIdField = $this->_entityIdField;
  $this->_entityIdField = 'entity_id';
  $resource = Mage::getSingleton('core/resource');
  $this->_write = $resource->getConnection('core_write');
  $this->_read = $resource->getConnection('core_read');
  parent::_updateAttribute($object, $attribute, $valueId, $value);
  $this->_entityIdField = $cmsEntityIdField;
  unset($this->_write);
  unset($this->_read);
  $this->_write = $cmsWrite;
  $this->_read = $cmsRead;
  return $this;
}
```

Do this for the `saveAttribute` method as well, switching the parent call to
`parent::saveAttribute($object, $attributeCode)`.

Inserting Attributes

The `_insertAttribute` method isn't as nice to override because of the update and
save methods, but it is shorter than the previous update method change. The
`_insertAttribute` method assumes that the name of the primary key for our attribute
tables is the same as our main entity table, but this isn't the case. So, we must force
the name `entity_id` as our primary field name, and we also want to use whatever
connection is configured for the customer module, not our own.

```
//force attributes back into M
protected function _insertAttribute($object, $attribute, $value)
{
    $entityIdField = 'entity_id';
    $row = array(
        $entityIdField  => $object->getId(),
        'entity_type_id'=> $object->getEntityTypeId(),
        'attribute_id'  => $attribute->getId(),
        'value'         =>
          $this->_prepareValueForSave($value, $attribute)
```

```
    );
    $resource = Mage::getSingleton('core/resource');
    $w = $resource->getConnection('customer_write');
    $w->insert($attribute->getBackend()->getTable(), $row);
    return $this;
}
```

Loading Attributes

We face the same problem with loading attributes. There is no clean way to override this code. This should prove as a good argument for the pattern of always naming your primary field as the table name plus _id.

```
//force attributes back into M
protected function _getLoadAttributesSelect($object, $table)
{
    $select = $this->_read->select()
        ->from($table)
        ->where('entity_id' . '=?', $object->getId());
    return $select;
}
```

Finally, the entity's own load method must be overridden to switch the resource when loading the entity's own attributes. Copy the entire load method from Mage/Eav/Model/Entity/Abstract.php into your entity class. We only have to change the bottom portion of this method, the part that loads the attributes.

```
/**
 * Load data for entity attributes
 */
$resource = Mage::getSingleton('core/resource');
$r = $resource->getConnection('core_read');
foreach ($this->getAttributesByTable() as $table=>$attributes) {
    $select = $this->_getLoadAttributesSelect($object, $table);
    $values = $r->fetchAll($select);
    foreach ($values as $valueRow) {
        $this->_setAttribteValue($object, $valueRow);
    }
}
```

Registration

We can now use your CMS database for logging into Magento. What we cannot do (still) is register on the Magento registration page. Saving any customer information, other than the default billing and shipping IDs, has not been implemented in our code. We have to make a decision about how our two sites integrate. If we allow registrations on Magento, we have to duplicate the same data validation and notification e-mails as the CMS registration process.

Also, we have to handle saving and updating of the values that we have pulled from the CMS: email, password, first name, and last name. We could do this in the entity's _beforeSave or _afterSave methods. Our other option is to add more eav_attribute entries for these fields, and perform checks in the _insertAttribute and _updateAttribute methods to choose which table and database connection to save the attribute values.

One option to avoid piling more code onto our solution is to simply remove the registration page from Magento and change all the links to point to our existing CMS registration process. There isn't a compelling argument to have two separate registration processes as you would have to keep two sets of registration logic in sync and bug free in two systems.

Another option to avoid two sets of logic is to integrate the CMS's registration process into Magento's by including libraries and code inside an overridden Magento controller.

Conclusion

After making all the code changes suggested above, you should be able to login to Magento with a username and password from another database system, most likely a flat table structure. With this account you can change your address book, choose your default addresses, and place an order. As discussed previously, we cannot modify any information in the CMS's database without doubling our coding efforts. A lot of work went into this solution, but it simplifies all the ongoing maintenance of a solution which publishes information to two separate spots, and gives the end user a seamless shopping experience.

Synchronizing Sessions

Even though our two databases are now sharing login information, we are still not allowing a user to log-in on one site and still be logged in when they visit the other. Both sites must be located on the same domain for this solution to work, as it involves sending two session cookies from both the CMS and Magento.

Magento Listeners

Magento's event listener system can be used to trigger a custom method in our User-Connect module. Let's make a Helper/Login.php file to serve as our helper. The code is quite small for both of these methods.

```
class Company_UserConnect_Helper_Login
  extends Mage_Core_Helper_Abstract
{
    /**
     * Start a session
     */
    static function loginEvent($observer) {
        $event = $observer->getEvent();
        //calling code
        //  Mage::dispatchEvent('customer_login',
        //    array('customer'=>$customer));
        $customer = $event->getCustomer();
        $customerId = $customer->getId();
        $cgnUser = Cgn_User::load($customerId);
        $cgnUser->bindSession();
    }
}
```

You can see that the loginEvent grabs the $event object off of the passed in observer. I have commented the Magento code that triggers this event so you can see what parameters are passed along - the customer object - and the name of the event = customer_login.

The bindSession method and Cgn_User objects are specific to my own framework, Cognifty. It should be no trouble for you to replace the two lines of code with session initializing code from whatever CMS you are already working with. Remember to *include* or *require* any necessary libraries.

```
/**
 * Destroy a session
 */
static function logoutEvent($observer) {
    $event = $observer->getEvent();
    //calling code
    //  Mage::dispatchEvent('customer_login',
    //    array('customer'=>$customer));
    $customer = $event->getCustomer();
    $customerId = $customer->getId();
    $cgnUser = Cgn_User  load($customerId);
    $cgnUser->unBindSession();
}
```

The logoutEvent follows the style of the loginEvent. To activate these methods, we must add some XML to the config.xml file for our UserConnect module.

```
...
<frontend>
...
  <events>
    <customer_login>
      <observers>
        <userconnect_login>
          <type>model</type>
          <class>Company_UserConnect_Helper_Login</class>
          <method>loginEvent</method>
        </userconnect_login>
      </observers>
    </customer_login>
...
```

The events tag falls under the frontend tag. The next tag is the name of the event we would like to listen to, in this case it's customer_login. The observers tag defines a list of the classes and methods which we would like to have triggered whenever the event in question is fired. We must give our event observer a name, it doesn't matter what the name is as long as it is unique. It is probably best to prepend this name with a module name to guarantee uniqueness amongst all the listeners for the system.

The class and method tags should be self explanatory. The type tag can be one of *singleton* or *model.* For most event listeners, the distinction between the two choices is not noticeable.

The configuration for the logout event listener is almost identical to the login listener, except for the name of the observer: `userconnect_logout` and the name of the method.

```
...
<frontend>
...
    <customer_logout>
      <observers>
        <userconnect_logout>
          <type>model</type>
          <class>Company_UserConnect_Helper_Login</class>
          <method>logoutEvent</method>
        </userconnect_logout>
      </observers>
    </customer_logout>
  </events>
...
```

CMS Sessions

To fully finish the integration, we need to modify the content system's login method to start a Magento session. The structure of this code will be heavily dependent on how your chosen framework or CMS handles modules, plugins, etc. Again, this example uses the Cognifty framework as I can speak with authority on its functionality. The example code is also slimmer than any example using other popular content management systems.

```
class Cgn_Slot_Magento {

    function bindMagentoToSession($signal) {
        $source = $signal->getSource();
        $user = $source->user;

        include('magento/app/Mage.php');
        Mage::app('base');
        $customer = Mage::getModel('customer/customer');
        $customer->loadByEmail($user->email);
        $session = Mage::getSingleton('customer/session');
        $session->start();
```

```
            $session->setCustomer($customer);
    }
}
```

Shared Themes

As a final *pièce de résistance* to our integration methods, we will cover how to re-use an existing CMS theme or template to wrap Magento's core output. Magento's layout system is built as a set of nested blocks. We can inspect the layout, grab the core content block, and throw away the rest of the layout. Plugging in this output into our content system's templating system results in a fairly nice result.

Care must be taken to include all of Magento's CSS and Javascript dependencies on our existing theme.

```
function mainEvent(&$req, &$t) {
    ob_end_clean();
    //Start Magento
    Mage::app('default');
    //don't automatically send output
    $controller = Mage::app()->getFrontController()->setNoRender(true)->
        dispatch();
    //*do* send output
    $controller->setNoRender(false);
    //don't start output at the root layout block
    $controller->getAction()->getLayout()->removeOutputBlock('root');
    //*do* start output at the content layout block
    $controller->getAction()->getLayout()->addOutputBlock('content');
    $controller->getAction()->renderLayout();
    $t['mage_output'] = $controller->getResponse()->__toString();
}
```

Store Driven Integration

In this chapter we have reviewed how to integrate a CMS into Magento with a style that I call "CMS driven" integration. The flip-side of this style would be "store-driven" integration, in which Magento takes center stage and all methods and pages default to Magento, instead of the CMS.

Store driven integration will not be covered in this book. Store driven integration really makes the most sense for new sites or communities which do not have an existing user-base. Given Magento's ability to create static and dynamic pages, integrating in a plain CMS which has no native ability to extract product information from Magento has limited appeal.

Chapter 8

Made to Order Module

In Magento, everything you wish to sell must be defined as a *Simple Product* having its own SKU and price. But there are times when a merchant wishes to sell items that do not have a unique identifying code, like a SKU. The reason that some products might not have an identifying SKU depend largely on the type of item being sold and the organization of the merchant's business.

These types of situations are especially common for manufacturers who take special orders for items that they may only make one time. An example that most anybody can relate to would be purchasing produce or meat at a supermarket. Apples are sold by the pound, purchasing one pound of apples costs more than purchasing a half pound of apples, or any fractional weight in between. But, each possible weight of apples does not have its own predetermined and unique SKU number. The type of apple probably has a unique *PLU*, or Price Look-Up code, but the final item of the transaction is an item and a specific quantity; weight in this example.

This fabricated receipt shows an example of how individual line-items of a receipt can be composed of a dimension or quantity plus a unique identifying number, such as a SKU or PLU.

```
Sample receipt print-out of buying apples.

0.5 @ $3.00 / lbs
........ 1200 Red Apples .......... $1.50
```

```
3.19 @ $2.00 / lbs
........ 2200 Florida Oranges ...... $6.38

------------------------------------

Sub-Total ........................ $7.88
```

Magento currently lacks the ability to accept user input as a determining factor for the end result of a transaction. The customer can only pick from a predetermined selection of items. For manufacturers, who might take special orders for products with varying dimensions of size, this could result in Magento's database containing millions of "products". The management of such a database would become cumbersome, in part because it is not how the manufacturer thinks about their own products.

Example Scenario

The best example situation where a user's input would affect the price is choosing the size of an item. Let's pretend that you work for a manufacturer of rain gutters and you need to implement a shopping cart which allows the customer to enter the quantity and length of each desired piece. A customer who needs gutters for the front and back of his thirty foot wide house might order:

- 1 x 30 foot piece

- 3 x 5 foot pieces

- 2 x 12.5 foot pieces

Obviously we would like to record the length required for each piece as part of each line-item on the order. We would also like the length to determine the price for each piece. Although possible, it would not be the best option to enter an individual product for every available fractional length. Not only would you have hundreds of products for each style of gutter, imagine trying to update the price because the cost of raw materials increased.

Plan of Attack

In order to implement user input as part of our order, we need to understand how the order process works. When a user adds a product to their cart, a *quote item* is created from the product and that quote item is what is added to the user's cart, not the product itself. When the user completes the order, the quote, and all of its items are transformed into an order. Just like adding attributes to a product, we can add new attributes to *quote items* and *order items*. Although there is no user interface for this task, the concept is the same.

- Create a new attribute for length products

- Create a new attribute for quote items

- Create a new attribute for order items

- Create a new product template to get length input

- Add event listeners to the order process to alter the quote and order items

- Alter the checkout screen to show the length attribute

The Length Attribute

Creating this new attribute does not affect the code of our new module. We will simply create a new product attribute using the admin interface. Create a new product attribute called `mto_length`. This attribute will not be visible on the front end, and it does not require any special validation. The input type should be `Yes/No` for the store owner. All we want to do with this attribute is to signal the various blocks and templates to show new inputs to the user (Figure 8.1).

When editing the product itself, we will only have a `Yes/No` choice for our gutter products (Figure 8.3).

New Module

Start by create a shell module called `Mto`. The process for creating a shell module is described in the *Custom Modules* chapter. For this module, we will be using the `sql`

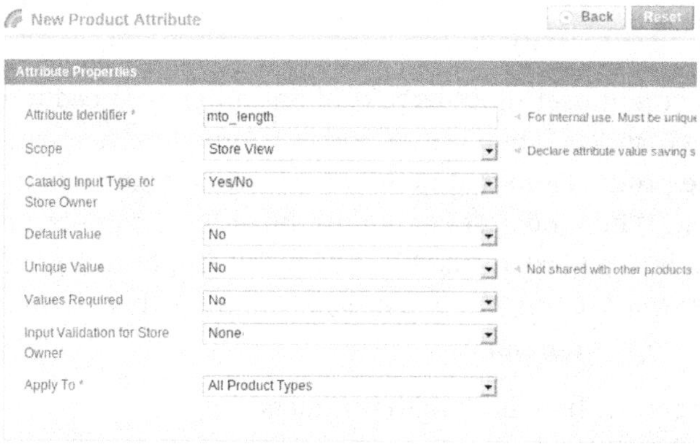

Figure 8.1

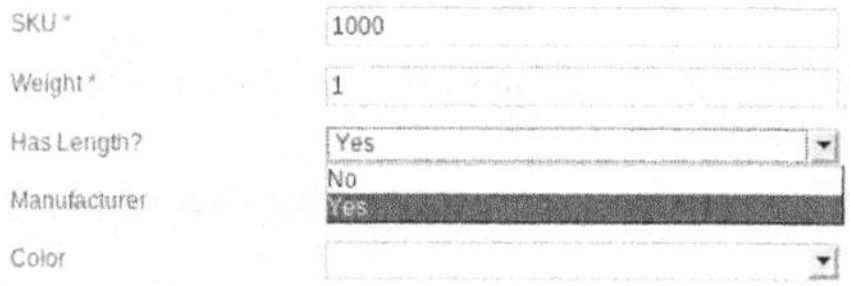

Figure 8.2

directory to add new attributes to the database. We will also be overriding Magento blocks and models, as well as creating a helper class for event listening purposes.

Installation

As described in the *Custom Modules* chapter, a module can run any SQL it needs when it is first installed, or when it is upgraded. In order to add new attributes to the order items and quote items, we need to create some new *eav_attribute* entries. Add this PHP code to your mysql4-install-0.1.0.php file.

```php
$c = array (
    'entity_type_id'=>$quote_type_id,
    'attribute_code'=>'mto_length',
    'backend_type'=>'varchar',
    'frontend_input'=>'text',
    'is_global' => '1',
```

```
        'is_visible' => '0',
        'is_required' => '0',
        'is_user_defined' => '1',
    );
```

This array defines all the values needed to create a new *eav_attribute* record. Copy this code twice, but change `quote_type_id` to `order_type_id` in the second instance. We need to create the `mto_length` attribute for both quotes and orders. I'll explain where the values of the `type_id` variables come from later.

```
$attribute = new Mage_Eav_Model_Entity_Attribute();
$attribute->loadByCode($c['entity_type_id'],$c['attribute_code'])
  ->setStoreId(0)
  ->addData($c);
$attribute->save();
```

This code creates a new attribute object, and loads it from the database if it exists already with the same *attribute_code*. Setting the store ID to *0* is required for single store installations. For multi-store installations, repeat this process for each store ID.

We want to duplicate both of these code blocks twice, once for the *quote items* and once for the *order items*. To get the value of `$quote_type_id` and `$order_type_id` we need to inspect the database. Since these values are auto-increment ID fields, they could change per installation, but the entity codes do not change. We will use the values *quote_item* and *order_item* to get the ID values from the database. The following code should go **above** the rest of the code in your installation file.

```
$eid = $read->fetchRow('select
    entity_type_id
    from eav_entity_type
    where entity_type_code="quote_item"');
$quote_type_id = $eid['entity_type_id'];

$eid = $read->fetchRow('select
    entity_type_id
    from eav_entity_type
    where entity_type_code="order_item"');
$order_type_id = $eid['entity_type_id'];
```

The final installation file should look something like this:

```
$read = Mage::getSingleton('core/resource')
  ->getConnection('core_read');

$eid = $read->fetchRow('select ...  where entity_type_code="quote_item"');

$quote_type_id = $eid['entity_type_id'];

//repeat the above for "order_item" and "order_type_id"

$installer = $this;
$installer->startSetup();
$c = array (
   'entity_type_id'=>$quote_type_id,
   'attribute_code'=>'mto_length',
...
);

$attribute = new Mage_Eav_Model_Entity_Attribute();
$attribute->loadByCode($c['entity_type_id'],$c['attribute_code'])
  ->setStoreId(0)
  ->addData($c);
$attribute->save();

//repeat the above for "order_item" and "order_type_id"
$installer->endSetup();
```

Overriding the Block

We want to develop our new length input field in the most modular way possible. To accomplish this we will override the default *Product View* block and conditionally add our new template piece, which we will create as a new core/template type block.

```
class Company_Mto_Block_Product_View
  extends Mage_Catalog_Block_Product_View
{

    protected function _prepareLayout()
    {
        $lengthBlock = $this->getLayout()->addBlock('core/template', '
            length_product')
            ->setTemplate('mto/length_product.phtml');
        $this->setChild('length_product',$lengthBlock);
        return parent::_prepareLayout();
```

```
        }
    }
```

This code creates a new template *block* of the type `core/template`. This type is the most basic type of block you can create. Its sole purpose is to include a template file. It provides no custom display logic like other, more specific, block classes.

To implement our new block we need to modify the `layout/catalog.xml` file. You can make this change by creating a new layout file and referencing the block in question, see the *Custom Modules* chapter for more information on safely over-riding blocks. Change the type attribute of the block under `content` in the *catalog_product_view* tag.

```
<catalog_product_view>
...
    <reference name="content">
<!--
        <block type="catalog/product_view" name="product.info"
            template="catalog/product/view.phtml">
-->
        <block type="mto/product_view" name="product.info"
            template="catalog/product/view.phtml">
...
    </reference>
...
</catalog_product_view>
```

Now, we have our new *product view block*, and it creates a new child block, but this new block still will not show up on our product view page. We must specifically instruct the original product view template to output this new `length_product` block at a specific spot. We output child blocks within a template with the method `getChildHtml`. The original product view template is in `template/catalog/product/view.phtml`. The best place to add our new block output is directly under the `product_type_data` block. The `product_type_data` block shows specific information for each type of product: *Simple, Configurable,* and *Bundle.*

```
<?php echo $this->getChildHtml('product_type_data') ?>

//new block for products with length.
```

```php
<?php echo $this->getChildHtml('length_product') ?>
```

The final piece of the template puzzle is the `.phtml` file itself. We have already referenced it in the code as `mto/length_product.phtml`. This file is very simple, it simply displays an input field to accept the user's input. This file can be more advanced. By adding a specific block for length-type products we could inspect more properties about the current product, show a range of acceptable sizes, or even dynamically update the price with AJAX-style coding. For now, our template file will remain barebones.

```html
<br style="clear:left;"/>
<br />
Length: <input type="text" name="user_length" size="3"/>
```

You should now see this input box on the product view page. The length box should be just below the quantity box, like the screen shot show in Figure 8.3.

Figure 8.3

Recording User Input

To attach any input the user wants to add to their order, or any line-item of the order, we must attach the data to an attribute of the *quote item*. We can't attach the specific information to the product, because the product is universal to all customers; whereas *quote items* and *order items* are not universal.

Attaching information to the quote can be done easily with event listeners. To understand the listener's structure, we must understand a little about Magento's process of adding a product to your cart.

The controller file `Checkout/controllers/CartContoller.php` performs all the tasks of adding, editing, and deleting products from the cart. The *cart* is just a *quote* object, with associated *quote item* objects. Usually you can get the quote object from any object with the getQuote method call. Quote items are regularly re-populated with fresh database values from products. Anytime the quote is loaded, the products related to the quote items are loaded and the items' properties are refreshed from the database. This makes trying to dynamically alter the price of an ordered item more difficult than it should be. But that's okay, since our length attribute is from the customer, and not from a product. We could inject our code right in to the controller, but we can wait for the quote item to be created, if a product that is not in the cart yet.

Just before the cart is saved, we will attach the user input directly from the request object.

Adding Data to the Quote

In order to enable the event listener, we need to register the listener in the config.xml. I like to put my event listener code in Helper/Event.php, while most of Magento's core code uses Model/Observer.php. (See "observer pattern" in the Index for more on this topic.)

```
<config>
...
  <frontend>
    <events>
      <sales_quote_save_before>
        <observers>
          <my_cart_checker>
            <type>singleton</type>
            <class>Company_Mto_Helper_Event</class>
            <method>cartBeforeSave</method>
          </my_cart_checker>
        </observers>
      </sales_quote_save_before>
...
```

The code for the listener should go into Helper/Event.php. Your class should be named after your module and it should *extend* Mage_Core_Helper_Abstract. The only method which we need to implement is the one named in the config file; cartBeforeSave. The body of this method is listed below.

```
/**
 * Called from "sales_quote_save_before"
 */
static function cartBeforeSave($observer) {
    $event = $observer->getEvent();

    $req =  Mage::app()->getRequest();
    $items = $event->getQuote()->getItemsCollection();
    $mto_length = $req->get('user_length');
    $product_id = $req->get('product');
    if (!$mto_length && !$product_id) {
        //only run if the user is submitting
        // data to the cart controller.
        return;
    }
    foreach ($items as $item) {
        if ($item->getProductId() === $product_id) {
            if(!$item->getMtoLength()) {
                $item->setMtoLength($mto_length);
                break;
            }
        }
    }
}
```

After implementing this method in your listener, you should be able to add any product which has its own mto_length set to Yes in the admin to your cart with any length value you want. If you inspect your database you should see a value in sales_quote_item_varchar like shown in Figure 8.4.

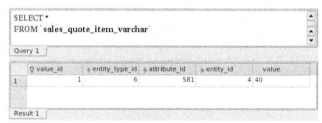

Figure 8.4

Adding Data to the Order

Even though we have successfully recorded the user input for this product, the data will not be saved to the order yet. For that, we need to implement one more event listener just before the order is saved. We can add one more method to our event helper to set certain order item attributes just before the order is committed to the database. Add the following code to your helper and activate it with XML similar to the previous event.

```
/**
 * Listens for "sales_convert_quote_item_to_order_item"
 */
static function attachSpecialOrderAttribs($observer) {

    $event = $observer->getEvent();
    $orderItem = $event->getOrderItem();
    $quoteItem = $event->getItem();

    $orderItem->setMtoLength( $quoteItem->getMtoLength() );
}



XML to activate the listener

<config>
...
  <frontend>
    <events>
...
      <sales_convert_quote_item_to_order_item>
       <observers>
         <my_order_attribs>
           <type>singleton</type>
           <class>Company_Mto_Helper_Event</class>
           <method>attachSpecialOrderAttribs</method>
         </my_order_attribs>
        </observers>
       </sales_convert_quote_item_to_order_item>
  ...
```

If you continue to purchase any product to which you've added a special length value, you should see the *mto_length* attribute in the database in the table `sales_order_entity_varchar` after the order is complete. The highlighted database row in Figure 8.5 shows an order with a customer value of 15 for the length of one section of gutter.

value_id ▼	entity_type_id	attribute_id	entity_id	value
109	13	382	18	
110	**13**	**582**	**18**	**15**
111	14	386	19	purchaseorder
112	14	389	19	
113	15	431	20	pending

Figure 8.5

Show Customizations to the Customer

Now that we have products available to the customer which aren't exactly represented in the database (i.e. of variable lengths) some parts of Magento don't quite look correct anymore. Take the cart page for example, if a customer adds two pieces of 30 foot gutter, and four pieces of 5 foot gutter, on the cart page we will simply see six pieces of gutter. We must divide this into two separate products, as well as show the user their own selected length for each item.

Modify the Cart Page

The cart page utilizes a method from the `checkout/cart` block to show an extra description for certain products. Only configurable products use this extra description method. The block method in question is called `getItemDescription` and takes a *quote item* as a parameter. This method acts as a facade for a *helper* event with a longer name; it simply passes the quote item parameter to the checkout module's data helper. We can take advantage of this fact by overriding the checkout data helper and inserting some logic to display our *mto length* attribute if necessary.

Override the checkout module's *data* helper by inserting the correct XML into our MTO module's `config.xml`. Then create a `Helper/Data.php` file which extends the original class `Mage_Checkout_Helper_Data`. The method name in question is `getQuoteItemProductDescription`. Now you can see why the cart block provides a façade for this method name. In the body of our overridden method we will defer to the parent method first, then add our custom logic afterwards.

```
class Company_Mto_Helper_Data
  extends Mage_Checkout_Helper_Data
{
    public function getQuoteItemProductDescription($item)
    {
        $desc = parent::getQuoteItemProductDescription($item);

        if ($item->getMtoLength()) {
            if ($desc !== '') {
                $desc .= '<br/>';
            }
            $desc .= 'Length: '.$item->getMtoLength().'\'';
        }
        return $desc;
    }
}
```

Separating Similar Products in the Cart

Because we are altering the cart contents in a way unexpected by Magento, the cart may not behave the way we expect. Currently, if we add two products with different length attributes, the cart will combine the two products together, as if we simply updated the quantity of the first product. We need to tell Magento that products with different length attributes are actually separate products. To do this we need to override the *quote* model from the *sales* module. This class contains getItemByProduct method which searches through the *quote items* already in the cart to find one that matches the product which the customer wants to add.

Magento's cart only matches *quote items* and products based on the product IDs. We need to override the getItemByProduct to compare a quote item's length against any posted length attribute from the request. Create a new Model/Sales/Quote.php file in your *Mto* module, make the class extend the original Mage_Sales_Model_Quote class.

```
//original code
  else {
      if ($item->getProductId() == $productId
        && is_null($superProductId)) {
        return $item;
      }
```

```
    }

//new code
 else {
     if ($item->getProductId() == $productId
         && is_null($superProductId)) {
         if ($item->getMtoLength()) {
             if ($item->getMtoLength() !== Mage::app()->getRequest()
                 ->get('user_length') ) {
                     return false;
                 }
         }
         return $item;
     }
 }
```

You should now be able to add two of the same product and as long as you have different length values entered for each, they will appear as separate products in the cart. Figure 8.6 shows what you might see.

Figure 8.6

Conclusion

We have seen, in this chapter, how to alter the order process to attach special attributes to any product. This feature is ideal for products that are available in many different sizes. It can be extended to allow for changing the price of the quote item as well. Changing the price dynamically allows for many more possibilities than just dimensions or length. Some ideas for future changes might include:

- Adding support for ranges of values

- Charging for engravings on products by the letter

- Accepting spreadsheets from the customer, charge for processing data from the file

- Collecting different shipping dates for individual products with a calendar widget

- Recording special preparation instructions for food items

Chapter 9

Points and Rewards Module

Rewarding repeat customers with discounts is a time-tested method of garnering customer loyalty. In America, credit card companies, airline companies, soft drink companies, book stores, and coffee shops are all examples of businesses that reward their customers with points that can be redeemed for discounts on their next purchase. Redeeming points doesn't just have to be for a discount on the customer's next purchase, some ideas for the redemption of points include:

- Buying into a raffle for one large prize

- Recognition on a community Web site by increasing the customer's status or rank

- Discounted shipping rates

- Free membership to special Web site areas (e.g. private forums)

- Increased priority for shipping or problem resolution

- Send free gifts with your company's logo imprinted on them

- (pens, bags, clocks, stress relievers, etc.)

We are going to build a simple points and rewards module for Magento that hooks into the coupon system of Magento to apply a discount to the customer's entire order. Using the coupon system will reduce the overall complexity of the module and require less customization of Magento's templates.

Plan of attack

We are going to build this module in stages, the first stage is simply to keep track of points as the customer places orders. The second stage is to let the customer view their total points in the *My Account* area. Then we will tackle the redemption part of the process by using dynamic coupon codes. Lastly we will deduct any points used during an order from the customer's points total.

- Add points to products

- Record points for each product ordered

- Show the customer's accumulated points in the *My Account* area

- Create a dynamic coupon that will adjust its savings based on customer input

- Update the customer's points upon checkout

Adding New Attributes to Products

In order to have different point values for each product we will use Magento's attribute system and create an attribute called *reward_points*. Create this new attribute in *Manage Attributes* section of the backend. Make sure the following settings are correct:

- Attribute Identifier: reward_points

- Score: store view

- Catalog Input Type: text field

- Input Validation for Store Owner: Integer Number

- Visible on Catalog Pages: yes

- Manage Labels/Options: Points

When creating this attribute we have two choices when it comes to the visibility of the points. Setting the attribute as visible on the frontend catalog will display the points as any other attribute of the product in the *Additional Information* section of the product view page. This is a decent default behavior, but some stores might want to integrate the points value of a product throughout the store catalog with custom templates. If you are looking to integrate points throughout your entire store as a promotion technique, you might want to set the attribute now to show on the frontend catalog. This does not completely restrict the value from ever showing on the catalog, it just means that it now requires some special code in order for the value to be loaded and shown in various templates. For this example we will leave the visibility on.

After creating the attribute, attach it to any attribute set that is in use by a product. Afterwards, edit the product and give it a sample point value, let's use *100* as our sample points value. See *figure 6.2* in the *Custom Modules* chapter for an example of adding a new attribute to a product.

You should now see the **Points** value on the product view page in the *Additional Information* section. If you don't see it, double check that your chosen product is enabled, and that when you saved the points value to the product that there weren't errors. Lastly, double check the visibility setting of the points attribute.

Creating a Shell Module

Initialize a new module called RewardPoints. Referring to the module as RewardPoints is much easier to say than PointsandRewards over and over. We want to start off with an SQL table, so the new module's config file needs to be ready to run an installation file. (See the *Magento Modules* chapter for a thorough introduction to modules and directory structures.) The new config.xml file should look like the following:

```
<?xml version="1.0"?>
<config>
    <modules>
```

```xml
        <Company_RewardPoints>
            <version>0.1.0</version>
            <depends>
                <Mage_Customer />
                <Mage_Checkout />
            </depends>
        </Company_RewardPoints>
    </modules>
    <global>
        <resources>
            <rewardpoints_setup>
                <setup>
                    <module>Company_RewardPoints</module>
                    <class>Mage_Core_Model_Resource_Setup</class>
                </setup>
                <connection><use>core_setup</use></connection>
            </rewardpoints_setup>
            <rewardpoints_write>
                <connection><use>core_write</use></connection>
            </rewardpoints_write>
            <rewardpoints_read>
                <connection><use>core_read</use></connection>
            </rewardpoints_read>
        </resources>
    </global>
</config>
```

This is the bare minimum configuration you need to have a module that runs and one which is installable automatically.

Recording Points Ordered

Recording points requires a place to store the values associated with a customer. Our first step will be to create an SQL table and a *model* class to keep track of the points from each order. The table will hold information about the current number of points in a customer's account, the maximum points accumulated and the total points spent. The SQL table definition that holds the points information can be created by inserting the SQL into the module's *sql* directory.

```php
<?php
$installer = $this;
```

```
$installer->startSetup();
$installer->run("
DROP TABLE IF EXISTS {$this->getTable('rewardpoints_account')};
CREATE TABLE {$this->getTable('rewardpoints_account')} (
  'rewardpoints_account_id' integer(10) unsigned NOT NULL auto_increment,
  'customer_id' integer(10) unsigned NOT NULL default '0',
  'store_id' smallint(5) unsigned NOT NULL default '0',
  'points_current' integer(10) unsigned NULL default '0',
  'points_received' integer(10) unsigned NULL default '0',
  'points_spent' integer(10) unsigned NULL default '0',
  PRIMARY KEY  ('rewardpoints_account_id'),
  KEY 'FK_catalog_category_ENTITY_STORE' ('store_id'),
  KEY 'customer_idx' ('customer_id')
) ENGINE=InnoDB DEFAULT CHARSET=utf8 COMMENT='Reward points for an account';
");
$installer->endSetup();
```

Place the above code into RewardPoints/sql/rewardpoints_setup/mysql4-install-0.1.0.php.
The next page load on your Magento installation should run the install file and
create the table for you.

Making a Model

In order for us to be able to access our any models of *RewardPoints*, we need to add
some XML to tell Magento the class prefix we want to use with our models. Add the
following code to your module's etc/config.xml inside the global tag.

```
...
    <global>
        <models>
            <rewardpoints>
                <class>Company_RewardPoints_Model</class>
            </rewardpoints>
        </models>
    </global>
...
```

Now, any call to Mage::getModel('rewardpoints/x') will return a class like
Company_RewardPoints_Model_X. Next we will create a model to load and save data
from the table. Create a Models directory in your module directory. Make a class
called Account.php in the Models folder and add the code below.

```php
<?php
class Company_RewardPoints_Model_Account
    extends Mage_Core_Model_Abstract {

    protected $customerId = -1;
    protected $storeId    = -1;
    protected $pointsCurrent  = NULL;
    protected $pointsReceived = NULL;
    protected $pointsSpent    = NULL;

    //public setters and getters for every attribute

    //save and load methods

    //add and subtract points methods
}
```

Model Methods

We won't go cover the creation of getters and setters here, but create them in the class on your own. The two methods that we want to concentrate on are *save* and *load*. The *load* usually takes two arguments, the some ID value and the name of the ID field. The *save* method takes no arguments.

We will have to get our own database connections and write the SQL directly. If we decided to use a resource model we would get automatic database saves, but the configuration and setup is more complicated. See the *Database* chapter for a review of models and resource models.

```php
public function save() {
    $connection = Mage::getSingleton('core/resource')
        ->getConnection('rewardpoints_write');
    $connection->beginTransaction();
    $fields = array();
    $fields['customer_id'] = $this->customerId;
    $fields['store_id'] = $this->storeId;
    $fields['points_current'] = $this->pointsCurrent;
    $fields['points_received'] = $this->pointsReceived;
    $fields['points_spent'] = $this->pointsSpent;

    try {
        $this->_beforeSave();
```

```php
        if (!is_null($this->rewardpointsAccountId)) {
            $where = $connection->quoteInto('customer_id=?',
                $fields['customer_id']);
            $connection->update('rewardpoints_account',
                $fields, $where);
        } else {
            $connection->insert('rewardpoints_account', $fields);
            $this->rewardpointsAccountId =
                $connection->lastInsertId('rewardpoints_account');
        }
        $connection->commit();
        $this->_afterSave();
    }
    catch (Exception $e) {
        $connection->rollBack();
        throw $e;
    }
    return $this;
}


public function load($id, $field=null) {
    if ($field === null) {
        $field = 'customer_id';
    }
    $connection = Mage::getSingleton('core/resource')
        ->getConnection('rewardpoints_read');
    $select = $connection->select()
        ->from('rewardpoints_account')
        ->where('rewardpoints_account.'.$field.'=?', $id);
    $data = $connection->fetchRow($select);
    if (!$data) {
        return $this;
    }

    $this->setRewardpointsAccountId(
        $data['rewardpoints_account_id']
    );
    $this->setCustomerId($data['customer_id']);
    $this->setStoreId($data['store_id']);
    $this->setPointsCurrent($data['points_current']);
    $this->setPointsReceived($data['points_received']);
    $this->setPointsSpent($data['points_spent']);

    $this->_afterLoad();
```

```
        return $this;
    }
```

Notice the difference in preference of "id" fields between the `load` and `save` methods, the `save` method checks the table's primary key, but the `load` uses the `customer_id` field by default. You will probably have direct access to the `customer_id` value when trying to access a customer's points, but not the usually the row's primary key.

While developing this or any module, you will probably want to test the system iteratively. Setting up an entire controller, and template just to see if you've written your code correctly is overkill, you can include a simple shell script to load up Magento and execute just the methods of your model. See the last chapter for a detailed explanation of writing a shell method. For now, you can place this code in your module's directory, not the `chdir()` call to move the execution point back to Magento's main directory.

```php
<?php
chdir('..//..//..//../');
require_once 'app/Mage.php';
umask(0);
Mage::app('default');

$points = Mage::getModel('rewardpoints/account');
$points->load(1);
$points->save();
$points->save();
$points->save();
$points->load(3, 'rewardpoints_account_id');
var_dump($points);
```

Just two more simple methods and we'll be done with our model. We will be adding two utility methods to help keep track of the total points received and the total points spent.

```php
public function addPoints($p) {
    $this->pointsCurrent += $p;
    $this->pointsReceived += $p;
}

public function subtractPoints($p) {
```

```
        $this->pointsCurrent -= $p;
        $this->pointsSpent -= $p;
    }
```

Event Listeners

So far, our new module doesn't do very much other than install itself. We can load and save models, but only with our own test code. To record the points with each order we can simply write a function that listens to a Magento event that is fired every time an order is complete. For this we will need to add some XML to our module's etc/config.xml.

```xml
<config>
...
    <frontend>
        <events>
            <sales_order_place_after>
                <observers>
                    <recordOrderPoints>
                        <type>singleton</type>
                        <class>rewardpoints/observer</class>
                        <method>recordPointsForOrderEvent</method>
                    </recordOrderPoints>
                </observers>
            </sales_order_place_after>
        </events>
    </frontend>
...
</config>
```

The XML for listening to events falls under the *frontend* tag. You can also listen for events specifically when they are fired in the admin by putting the same XML under the *admin* tag. Under the *events* tag we list the actual names of the events that we want to listen to. Then we create our *observer* and give it any unique name with another XML tag. In this example our unique name is *recordOrderPoints*. This has no effect on your code. The type can either be *model* or *singleton*. A *model* type observer will be instantiated fresh before each call to the method. A *singleton* type observer is only created once no matter how many events it listens to or how many times an event is fired per request. The *class* tag specifies your *model* in the usual Magento short-hand syntax. The *method* tag should be self-explanatory.

The usual class name that Magento's own code uses for all event listeners is ModuleName/Model/Observer.php. This author likes to store event listeners in ModuleName/Helper/Event.php. The difference in the class name is minor, but the differences between event listener patterns and observer patterns is pretty distinct. An *observer/observable* pattern usually doesn't involve a third party event dispatcher, the observing object usually has a direct reference to the observable code. One other difference is that in event systems, or signal-slot systems, the events are have specific names, but in an observer/observable pattern the observer simply waits for one standard method call, like update().

For this example, we will tow the line and use the Model/Observer.php naming convention. Create a class in your module's Model directory that looks like the following code:

```php
<?php
class Company_RewardPoints_Model_Observer
  extends Mage_Core_Model_Abstract {

    /**
     * Record the points for each product.
     *
     * @triggeredby: sales_order_place_after
     * @param $eventArgs array "order"=>$order
     */
    public function recordPointsForOrderEvent($observer) {
        $order = $observer->getEvent()->getOrder();
        $items =$order->getItemsCollection();

        //load all products for each sales item

        //sum up points per product per quantity

        //record points for item into db
    }
}
```

The method recordPointsForOrderEvent should match the value of the *method* tag in your event XML. Each event listening method receives one argument: $observer.

For most every case, the only thing you want to do is retrieve the *event* from the observer with getEvent(). The event object contains a variable number of arguments depending on the code that triggered the event. You can print out the array keys of $event->getData() or search for the event producing code and see which exact variables are included as arguments.

To finish off the recordPointsForOrderEvent method add the following code under the comments.

```
//grab the customerId
$customerId = Mage::getModel('customer/session')
    ->getCustomerId();

//load all products for each sales item
$rewardPoints = 0;
$prodIds = array();
foreach ($items as $_item) {
    $prodIds[] = $_item->getProductId();
}
//load products from quote IDs to get the points
//(this won't work if points were set dynamically
//  in the addToCart process)

$prod = Mage::getResourceModel('catalog/product_collection')
    ->addAttributeToSelect('reward_points')
    ->addIdFilter($prodIds);


//sum up points per product per quantity
foreach ($items as $_item) {
    $rewardPoints += $prod->getItemById($_item->getProductId())
        ->getRewardPoints() * $_item->getQtyOrdered();
}


//record points for item into db
$this->recordPoints($rewardPoints, $customerId);
```

For the saving of points we will segment the code into another method. The recordPoints method will be well defined with 2 inputs, the total points and the customer's ID. What we lose here is the tracking of points per individual item, but the loss of this history should be acceptable for our purposes.

```
public function recordPoints($pointsInt, $customerId) {
    $points = Mage::getModel('rewardpoints/account')
        ->load($customerId);
    $points->addPoints($pointsInt);
    $points->save();
}
```

Summary

We have completed the first 2 steps in our plan of attack for this module. Now you should be able to complete a real order with any product that you have added points to. The points should accumulate in our new database table. Double check that the points are saving by peeking at MySQL and looking at our `rewardpoints_account` table. Assuming that you can see the points correctly in the database, we need to allow the customer to see their points.

Show the Customer Their Points

Now that we have the points saving properly, we need to show the customer how many points they have. We will add a simple box the account dashboard—Figure 9.1 shows an example of what we want to dashboard to look like.

Dashboard Layout

To add our own box to the customer's account dashboard we need to make a copy of the current dashboard template, create a new template that shows our points information, and create a new layout XML file to inject our new template file into the copied dashboard template. It is pretty important to understand why we have to make 3 copies to get 1 change into the template.

The dashboard page is composed of a dashboard.phtml which includes a few other parts into itself. We have to make a copy of this file so we can specify that we also want it to include our points template file. Even if we just wanted to write some

Figure 9.1

PHP directly into the dashboard file, instead of following the pattern that Magento has done by segmenting portions of the dashboard into include files, we would still want to make a copy of the dashboard file to avoid conflicts when upgrading.

Our layout file will only include enough instructions to change the current dashboard template file to our own, and to initialize a new block that will parse our points template file. Remember that all template files have a parent *block* which owns them. You can avoid writing a new class file for every template you use by calling on an existing block, like `core/template`, to simply parse any `.phtml` file you want. But you cannot directly inject a `.phtml` file anywhere into the layout without some kind of block owning it.

When you write a module for Magento, there is no default place to save your template files or layout file changes. We will create a new directory under our module called `design`. This will hold two more directories, `templates` and `layout`. Now we have all of our work saved into one directory for easy packaging or CVS or SVN committing. This way, we don't files for our module spread out all over the Magento installation.

Now we will create our module's layout XML file, save this file as `RewardPoints/design/layout/rewardpoints.xml`.

```
<?xml version="1.0"?>
<layout>
<!--
Customer account home dashboard layout
-->
```

```
<customer_account_index>
    <reference name="customer_account_dashboard">
        <action method="setTemplate">
            <template>rewardpoints/my_dashboard.phtml</template>
        </action>
        <block type="core/template"
               name="customer_account_points"
               as="points"
               template="rewardpoints/dashboard_points.phtml"/>
    </reference>
</customer_account_index>
</layout>
```

The tag *customer_account_index* is taken from the customer.xml layout file, which
defines the base screen that we see when we login to the My Account page. If
you examine the customer.xml file you will see where the reference name comes
from for the value customer_account_dashboard. What the above XML configuration does is reset the main template for that block to our new template,
my_dashboard.phtml, and adds a new core template type block as a new child of the
customer_account_dashboard block. The core template type block provides only the
base template functionality, so we won't have any specialized display logic available
to us inside the dashboard_points.phtml file.

Now, we must copy the original dashboard file to our templates directory (our template directory under the main design directory, not to our module's design directory). Then, we can simply add one call to tell the system to parse our new child
block called points. The original dashboard file can be found under the default design directory at template/customer/account/dashboard.phtml.

```
<div class="page-head">
    <h3><?php echo $this->__('My Dashboard') ?></h3>
</div>
<?php echo $this->getMessagesBlock()->getGroupedHtml() ?>
<?php echo $this->getChildHtml('hello') ?>
<?php echo $this->getChildHtml('top') ?>

<div class="account-box ad-account-info">
    <div class="head">
        <h4><?php echo $this->__('Points') ?></h4>
    </div>
<?php echo $this->getChildHtml('points') ?>
```

```
</div>
```

The above code is only a portion of the dashboard template, but the last *div* is the entirety of what we need to add to it. The last file which we need to write is the actual template to display the points. We've already added this to the layout, and we've told our new dashboard file to display the contents of this file with the getChildHtml('points') method. Put the following code into templates/rewardpoints/dashboard_points.phtml. Remember to clear Magento's cache if you are having problems seeing changes in the system, and hopefully you've remembered to create all the getters and setters in the *Account* model.

```php
<?php
$customerId = Mage::getModel('customer/session')->getCustomerId();
$customerPoints = Mage::getModel('rewardpoints/account')
    ->load($customerId);
?>
Your  Points: <?= sprintf('%d',
        $customerPoints->getPointsCurrent()); ?>
<br/>

Total Points Accumulated: <?= sprintf('%d',
        $customerPoints->getPointsReceived()); ?>
<br/>

Total Points Spent: <?= sprintf('%d',
        $customerPoints->getPointsSpent()); ?>
<br/>
```

Summary

If all goes well you should be seeing a page similar to the one presented at the beginning of this section. Now we have completed the third step in our plan of attack for this module. The last two steps are just as easy as the first three.

Dynamic Coupons

The idea for redeeming your coupons is that the customer applies however many points they want to their final order just like a coupon. Magento already has a coupon system built-in, but the problem is that we want to accept a variable number of points from users. The current Magento coupon system requires that you define every possible coupon code. Our plan for this section is to create 1 coupon for points, define some basic rules, and hijack the coupon system to dynamically alter the value of discount.

By piggy-backing off of the existing coupon system we gain a lot of advantages:

- The coupon submission is already part of the template

- There already exists a controller to handle applying discounts to orders

- The existing rules can perform percentage or dollar amount discounts

- The existing rule structure has start and stop dates

- The rules can be limited to applying coupons to certain SKUs only.

All these existing features make the coupon system a good choice to start our coupon redemption phase. In order to get these benefits from the coupon system, we have to create a coupon code first. Let's make a discount with the coupon code `points`. Whenever the customer wants to use their points, they will enter `points100` as the coupon code to apply 100 of their earned points towards the current order. When creating our one and only discount rule, we can specify a percentage discount, or a flat dollar discount. For now, we will go with a flat dollar discount and make each `point` worth one cent.

From the above figure you can see that there are a number of discount methods available. The names are a bit confusing, the percentage one takes off a percentage of any matching SKU, or the entire order if no SKU is specified. For our example, we'll choose *Fixed amount for whole cart*.

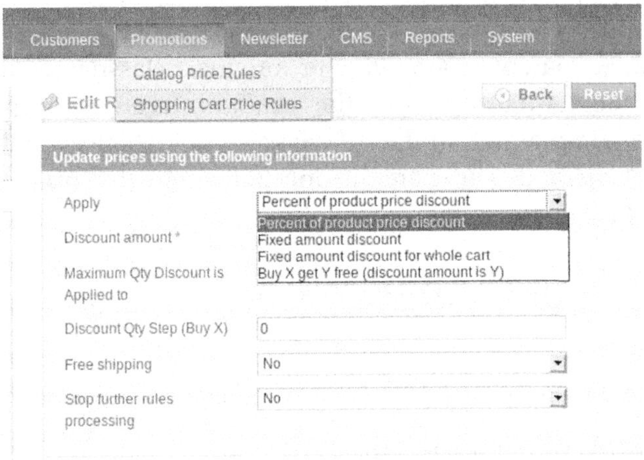

Figure 9.2

Coupon Models

To start, we need to copy two models into our module, change their class-name, and write some XML to set them as override models. Start by copying `Mage/SalesRules/Model/Rule.php` and `Mage/SalesRules/Model/Validator.php` to our module. Next, add the following XML into our `etc/config.xml` file:

```xml
...
  <global>
...
  <models>
    <salesrule>
      <rewrite>
        <rule>Company_RewardPoints_Model_Rule</rule>
        <validator>Company_RewardPoints_Model_Validtor</validator>
      </rewrite>
    </salesrule>
  </models>
...
  </global>
...
```

Now, rename the classnames to match the prefix `Company_RewardPoints_` and change their parent class to the original classname (i.e. extends `Mage_SalesRule_Model_Validtor`). In the *validator* class we can delete everything except the `init` method. In the *rule* class we can delete everything except the `getDiscountAmout` method. These are the only 2 methods that we need to modify in order to `hijack` the coupon system.

```
class Company_RewardPoints_Model_Validator
      extends Mage_SalesRule_Model_Validator
{

  public function init($websiteId, $customerGroupId, $couponCode)
  {
    $this->setWebsiteId($websiteId)
     ->setCustomerGroupId($customerGroupId)
     ->setCouponCode($couponCode);

    if ( substr($couponCode,0,6) === 'points') {
      $codeName = 'points';
      $pointsAmt = substr($couponCode,6);
    } else {
      $codeName = $couponCode;
      $pointsAmt = 0;
    }

    $this->_rules = Mage::getResourceModel('salesrule/rule_collection')
     ->setValidationFilter($websiteId, $customerGroupId, $codeName)
     ->load();
    foreach ($this->_rules as $_rule) {
      if ($_rule->getCouponCode() == 'points') {
        $_rule->setCouponCode($couponCode);
        $_rule->setPointsAmt($pointsAmt);
      }
    }
    return $this;
  }
}
```

In our extended validator we are overriding the `init` method to transform the coupon code. If we get a user submitted coupon code that has the word "points" in it, then we will trick the system into loading the "points" discount rule. But, we will also reset the rule's name to the original, user submitted, coupon code so that it has access to the original user input for later checking or double checking.

```
class Company_RewardPoints_Model_Rule
    extends Mage_SalesRule_Model_Rule
{

    public function validate(Varien_Object $object) {
        if (substr($this->getCouponCode(),0,6) != 'points') {
          return parent::validate($object);
        }

        $customerId = Mage::getModel('customer/session')
          ->getCustomerId();
        $points = Mage::getModel('rewardpoints/account')
          ->load($customerId);

        $current = $points->getPointsCurrent();

        if ($current < $this->getPointsAmt()) {
          Mage::getSingleton('checkout/session')->addError(
            'Not enough points available.'
          );
          return false;
        }
        return true;
    }

    public function getDiscountAmount() {
        if (substr($this->getCouponCode(),0,6) == 'points') {
            return ($this->getPointsAmt() / 100);
        }
        return parent::getDiscountAmount();
    }
}
```

In our extended rule class, we need to address 2 issues. The first one is, does the user have enough points to cover what they requested to use? This is done in the *validate* method. The second issue is, what is the current value of the coupon? The value is figured out dynamically by dividing the points by 100. This should give us a reasonable 1% discount for each 100 points. Obviously, the math is going to rely heavily on how many points you have assigned to your own products.

Deducting Points

Now, we are at the last section of our reward points module. The last thing we need to do is deduct points used by the customer upon checkout. We already have a listener setup to **add** points from products purchased, let's use that same listener (the Observer.php file) to deduct points that a user has spent.

```php
//add this to the very end of recordPointsForOrderEvent() in
//  Model/Observer.php

    //subtract points for this order
    if ($couponCode = $order->getCouponCode()) {
        $this->useCouponPoints($couponCode, $customerId);
    }

//this completely new method should be placed outside
// recordPointsForOrderEvent(), but inside the class

    public function useCouponPoints($couponCode, $customerId) {
        if ('points' !== substr($couponCode,0,6)) {
            return;
        }
        $pointsAmt = substr($couponCode,6);
        $points = Mage::getModel('rewardpoints/account')
            ->load($customerId);
        $points->subtractPoints($pointsAmt);
        $points->save();
    }
```

If done properly our event listener will add or subtract points gained or spent on each order.

Conclusion

We have seen how to build a simple reward points system for our customers. But there are still some areas that could benefit from improvement. There are a number of cosmetic changes that can be applied to the templates to better present the concept of points to the customer. We could modify the product info page to display the value of the points attribute in a more prominent manner. We could also give better instructions on the checkout page, or make a completely new block to accept reward points from the customer.

There are other ideas that could fit into a reward points system altogether. With a little work we could take turn this whole concept into a reseller system. Modifying the registration page, we could capture a reseller ID in the URL or ask the user, "Who referred you?". Upon checkout, the reseller gets points as a percentage of the total sale, not the customer. For this we wouldn't *need* points on the products at all, but we still could use them, if so desired.

Another area of improvement could be to create a log table of all the points transactions, `rewardpoints_log`. Then we would update the `rewardpoints_account` table with a sum of the transactions in the log table, instead of modifying the account table all the time. This would provide an audit trail, as well as the ability to track more information, like when points were added or spent, what type of action created the points (order, registration, referral, etc.), and maybe even an expiration date for the points.

Chapter 10

Backend Integration

Fulfilling your orders is a big part of selling online. After an order is accepted into Magento, or any shopping cart system, you have to package the order, ship the order, check for fraud, and collect the payments. You may find that the Web interface to managing orders in Magento is lacking. Perhaps you need a team of people scanning orders for fraud. Perhaps you need to send messages to other parties to complete your order: shipping partners or manufacturing partners. In any case, if the Web interface doesn't meet your needs you will have to move the data into another system.

The most straight-forward way to export data out of Magento's backend is to create a simple REST-style system that prints out XML. But, after processing an order, we also want to update order statuses. So, we will need a full CRUD system available via REST style URL patterns.

Starting a New Module

Let's start by creating a new module called `AdminRest` under our `Company` package. We need to give it a shell `config.xml` and enable the module in `app/etc/modules/`. See the *Magento Modules* chapter for a detailed explanation of the XML file formats. We are going to add the XML in the `config.xml` to allow our module to have its own URL. Anything matching the **frontName** `adminrest` in the URL will trigger a controller action in our module's controller directory.

```
<?xml version="1.0"?>
<config>
   <modules>
      <Company_AdminRest>
         <version>0.6.0</version>
      </Company_AdminRest>
   </modules>
   <admin>
       <routers>
           <adminrest>
               <use>admin</use>
               <args>
                   <module>Company_AdminRest</module>
                   <frontName>adminrest</frontName>
               </args>
           </adminrest>
       </routers>
   </admin>
</config>
```

The Controller

To make a new controller we must add the directory controllers to our module. This must be lower case, as controllers are included differently than models, blocks, and helpers. When requesting a module with no other parameters in the URL the default controller file name is IndexController.php. The default method name when no other parameters (other than the module name) are passed is indexAction.

```
<?php
class Company_AdminRest_IndexController
      extends Mage_Adminhtml_Controller_Action
{

    public function indexAction()
    {
        echo "Hello, World.";
    }
}
```

This is the ubiquitous Hello, World example. Pointing your browser at:

```
http://127.0.0.1/magento/index.php/adminrest/
```

...should result in a display of Hello, World.. Adjust the URL to whenever your development copy of Magento is installed. The index.php is optional, depending on your specific configuration, but its presence is always tolerated.

CRUD Controller

We want to design a controller that can support some simple CRUD operations. It may be tempting to think that we can make one controller that can handle all types of models in Magento, but the relationships between models can become quite complex, therefore we will make one controller for every type of data that has a complex relationship with other models. Think about the relationships between orders, line items, customers, addresses, and discounts, would it be sanely possible to design a URL structure that could flag whether or not to include all of these relationships on demand? Well, it is possible, but the decision making inside the controller would be just as complex and code heavy as making four or five independent controllers.

For starters, we will create an OrderController.php in the controllers folder.

```php
<?php
class Company_AdminRest_OrderController
    extends Mage_Adminhtml_Controller_Action
{
    public function readAction() {}

    public function updateAction() {}

    public function deleteAction() {}

    public function createAction() {}

    public function echoXmlArray($array) {}

    public function echoXmlString($msg, $errcode=-1) {}

    public function wrapXml($arr, &$xmlString, $tagName='item') { }
}
```

It is very easy to query the database for some records and spit them out as XML. Trying to organize PHP data structures in such a way that they can be presented as a set of nested XML tags is challenging. Here is an example of how we want our XML to show up.

```
<?xml version="1.0"?>
<orders>
  <order>
    <entity_id>1</entity_id>
    <...>...</...>
    <items>
      <item>
        <entity_id>1</entity_id>
        <...>...</...>
      </item>
    </items>
    <addresses>
      <address>
        <type>shipping</type>
        <...>...</...>
      <address>
    </addresses>
  </order>
</orders>
```

Read Action

For the task of printing XML we are going to use a nested array structure. Any set of arrays that should be nested **under** a parent XML tag will be prepended with the array key _entityChildren. To avoid the ugly hacks of trying to guess at the English language rules of pluralization, any tag whose sole purpose is to group lower tags will simply be appended with _col for *collection*. Below are the necessary, but evil, functions of dealing with arrays and XML in the most simplistic way.

```php
public function echoXmlArray($array) {
    echo "<?xml version=\"1.0\" ";
    echo "<orders>\n";
    $xmlString = '';
    foreach ($array as $_order) {
        echo $this->wrapXml($_order, $xmlString, 'order');
```

```
        }
        echo $xmlString;
        echo "</orders>";
    }

    public function wrapXml($arr, &$xmlString, $tagName='item') {
        $xmlString .= "<$tagName>\n";
        foreach ($arr as $fieldName => $fieldValue) {
            if ($fieldName === '_entityChildren') {
                foreach ($arr['_entityChildren'] as $type => $nodes) {
                    //the next line is optional, but produces
                    // a different structure
                    $xmlString .= '<'.$type.'_col>'."\n";

                    foreach ($nodes as $_node) {
                        $this->wrapXml($_node,$xmlString,$type);
                    }
                    //the next line is optional, but produces
                    // a different structure
                    $xmlString .='</'.$type.'_col>'."\n";
                }
                continue;
            }
            $fieldValue = "<![CDATA[$fieldValue]]>";
            $xmlString.= "<$fieldName>$fieldValue</$fieldName>\n";
        }
        $xmlString.= "</$tagName>\n";
    }
```

The *readAction* method is going to handle requests to :

```
http://127.0.0.1/magento/index.php/adminrest/order/read
```

This read method will pull a collection of orders, any related entities, and format the arrays into a format suitable for the echoXmlArray method. This method can have quite a bit of flexibility by reading URL parameters.

```
public function readAction() {
    $collection = Mage::getResourceModel('sales/order_collection')
        ->addAttributeToSelect('*');

    $status = $this->getRequest()->getParam('status');
    if ($status !== NULL) {
```

```
        $collection->addFieldToFilter('status', $status);
    }
    $collection->load()->getItems();

    $getItems = $this->getRequest()->getParam('items') !== NULL;
    $getAddr = $this->getRequest()->getParam('addresses') !== NULL;

    $collectionArray = $collection->toArray();
    foreach ($collectionArray as $_key => $_order) {
        $_order['_entityChildren'] = array();

        if ($getItems) {
            $_order['_entityChildren']['item'] =
                $collection->getItemById($_order['entity_id'])
                ->getItemsCollection()
                ->toArray();
            //write array back into place
            $collectionArray[$_key] = $_order;
        }

        if ($getAddr) {
            $_order['_entityChildren']['address'] =
                $collection->getItemById($_order['entity_id'])
                ->getAddressesCollection()
                ->toArray();
            //write array back into place
            $collectionArray[$_key] = $_order;
        }
    }
    $this->echoXmlArray($collectionArray);
}
```

What we see in the readAction method is the loading of an order collection object. Collection objects are a specialized way of dealing with multiple objects and are just about the only way to select items from the database with *where* clauses without writing raw SQL or using the Zend Framework *Select* object. The *status* parameter is read from the URL and, if it is present, is added as a filter to the collection object before it loads its orders.

In a similar manner, we can control which related data items we want to pull from the database by passing *items* and *addresses* parameters in the URL. These sub-items are not loaded from the collection object. Instead, as we are looping through the array of orders, trying to structure our data for XML output, if we see that items or addresses are requested we pull the order model out of the original collection and ask it to find its own collections of related items.

Lastly, we pass the organized and structured array to our echoXmlArray method. This loops through the items of the array, encoding every value in CDATA brackets, and recursively calls itself if it finds any _entityChildren.

Here is how this read action method might be called:

- index.php/adminrest/order/read/

- index.php/adminrest/order/read/status/pending/addresses/1

- index.php/adminrest/order/read/status/pending/addresses/1/items/1

Update Action

The next most common task after exporting the data to a third party tool is to update the data, most likely with a new status. When updating we probably want to update a lot of records at the same time, a batch update. The most critical part of batch updating is handling errors. Reporting errors to the invoking client is essential to the client's proper functioning.

When considering how to create this module, we are essentially creating an API for other clients to use. We must balance ease of use with functionality. Updating multiple properties of a record during each call is easy if we are only dealing with one record at a time. If we decide to accept a list of IDs and perform a batch update on multiple records, the error reporting that goes back to the client could be prohibitively complicated. The trade off of updating multiple records at a time but only one attribute at a time should form a good balance of flexibility and ease of use.

For our module, this will be our test URL.

- index.php/adminrest/order/update/a/status/v/processing/ids/1,2,3,4

The code for creating our update action looks like this.

```
public function updateAction() {
    $collection = Mage::getResourceModel('sales/order_collection')
        ->addAttributeToSelect('*');
```

```
$request = $this->getRequest();
$attribute = $request->getParam('a');
$attributeValue = $request->getParam('v');
if (!$attribute) {
    $this->echoXmlString('no attribute');
    return false;
}
$idList = explode(',', $request->getParam('ids'));
$collection->addFieldToFilter('entity_id', $idList);

$collection->load()->getItems();

$results   = array();
foreach ($collection as $_key => $_order) {
    $_order->setData($attribute, $attributeValue);
    try {
        $_order->save();
        $results[] = array('success'=>'yes', 'entity_id'=>$_order->getId
            ());
    }
    catch (Exception $e){
        $results[] = array('success'=>'no', 'entity_id'=>$_order->getId
            ());
    }
}
$this->echoXmlArray($results);
}
```

The create and delete methods round out our CRUD system. You should be able to easily copy the updateAction and change a few lines to make the createAction and deleteAction methods on your own.

Delete Action

For both the deleteAction and the updateAction we have two choices for implementing the database calls. We can send direct SQL statements to the database server for updating rows and deleting rows. The other way involves, as the example code demonstrates, loading objects individually and calling *save* after updating its attributes or calling *delete*. At first, the second method may seem like an unoptimized way to achieve the same results. But there is one difference. By loading each object individually, then calling *save* or *delete* we gain the advantage of calling system events and _afterSave and _beforeLoad model methods. This may not seem like such a great advantage, but you might not be sure which exact class is returned as a "sales/order" model. Any installed module has the ability to override that core model with its own sub-class which might be relying on the _afterSave or _beforeLoad methods.

Think about interaction with other modules while you are writing Magento code. If you are making a module for redistribution, don't assume that the target installation will not have any other models modifying the same data and methods that you are modifying.

The code for the deleteAction is almost identical to the update action, except we will call *delete* on the order instead of *save*.

```php
public function deleteAction() {
    $collection = Mage::getResourceModel('sales/order_collection');

    $request = $this->getRequest();
    $idList = explode(',', $request->getParam('ids'));
    if (!is_array($idList)) {
        $this->echoXmlString('no ids supplied');
        return false;
    }
    $collection->addFieldToFilter('entity_id', $idList);

    $collection->load()->getItems();

    $results = array();
    foreach ($collection as $_key => $_order) {
        try {
            $_order->delete();
            $results[] = array('success'=>'yes', 'entity_id'=>$_order->getId
                ());
        }
        catch (Exception $e){
            $results[] = array('success'=>'no', 'entity_id'=>$_order->getId
                ());
        }
    }
    $this->echoXmlArray($results);
}
```

Create Action

The createAction method allows us to create one order at a time. The argument list can become very long because of the amount of data required to create a valid order. We could probably make the argument list smaller by inserting some default data into the order object, like created_at, but this would reduce the flexibility of the API for some use cases. This method would probably be better suited to a POST call, rather than a GET HTTP request because of the amount of arguments involved. Luckily, this will not affect our code, unless we want to **enforce** the POST method to be used by the client.

```
index.php/adminrest/order/create/
POST data:
attr1=val1
attr2=val2
attr3=val3
...
```

After a successful creation we want to send the new entity_id back to the client. After a failure, we will return the message from any caught exception.

```
public function createAction() {
    $order = Mage::getModel('sales/order');
    $request = $this->getRequest();
    $params = $request->getParams();
    foreach ($params as $key => $value) {
        $order->setData($key, $value);
    }
    $results   = array();
    try {
        $order->save();
        $results[] = array('success'=>'yes',
                    'entity_id'=>$order->getId());
    }
    catch (Exception $e){
        $results[] = array('success'=>'no',
                    'message'=>$e->getMessage());
    }
    $this->echoXmlArray($results);
}
```

Securing the Controller

Currently, anyone is allowed to use our fancy, new CRUD controller. Securing our controller is pretty involved. Magento's `Mage_Adminhtml_Controller_Action` class does not give any security benefits. All the security settings come from the `Adminhtml` module. Since our module is not the `Adminhtml` module, we must hack together some security support ourselves.

A controller action's `preDispatch` method is called before every action method is called. Accordingly, we can inject some authentication into the `preDispatch` method.

Magento's core uses specialized events for handling access to the `Adminhtml` module. The code is not re-usable in a way where any module can enforce an admin login to access itself.

```
public function preDispatch() {
    parent::preDispatch();
    $session  = Mage::getSingleton('admin/session');
    $request = $this->getRequest();
    $user = $session->getUser();
    if (!$user) {
        $this->echoXmlString('no login');
        $request->setDispatched(FALSE);
    }
}
```

The code is fairly simple, the session either returns a valid and logged-in user or *NULL* from the `getUser` method. If the user is not present, we want to echo an XML response saying so. Since we are not using an advanced XML API like XML-RPC or SOAP, we have no standard way of suggesting to the client where the login controller is, like with an HTTP redirect header. We just hope that the client is reading our responses and will act accordingly to a "no login" error.

Calling `setDispatched(FALSE)` on the request stops any more processing of this request. The problem is that Magento uses this flag in two ways. Once a router matches a request URL to a controller, the router flags the request as "already dispatched". But the controllers use the flag in a different, and very specific, way. A controller's `preDispatch` method can basically unset the dispatch flag with `setDispatched(FALSE)`, but it **must** forward the request to a different module, controller, or action. Unsetting the dispatch flag stops the main action of a controller from executing, but the main front controller loops through **all** the routers again until a new match is found. If you don't forward the request (internally) to another controller, your preDispatch method will be called 100 times, even though your action methods are skipped. This strange logic is part of the reason why Magento handles its own security in a separate event. There just simply is no methodology for asking a matched controller if it should continue processing or not without throwing an exception. Throwing an exception is not a possibility for us since all output from a module is self-contained, that means that the core system has no idea that we always want to output XML, and therefore an exception would result in echoing the exception's message and a broken XML document to our client.

The overriding rule here is that for every request, at least one action method **must** be processed, or else you will end up cycling through all of your routers and controllers 100 times.

Let's look at our preDispatch method again after that lengthy explanation of Magento's internals. We are no going to incorporate a noaccessAction method to handle displaying anything we want when the user doesn't have an admin session.

```
public function preDispatch() {
    parent::preDispatch();
    $session  = Mage::getSingleton('admin/session');
    $request = $this->getRequest();
    $user = $session->getUser();
    if ($request->getActionName() !== 'noaccess') {
        if (!$user) {
            $request
                ->setControllerName('order')
                ->setActionName('noaccess')
                ->setDispatched(false);
        }
    }
}
```

Now, we are forwarding the request onto another action in the same order controller class. Remember that setting the dispatch flag to *false* does two things: skips main action execution, and recycles all routers to try matching again. If the request's action name is not yet set to *noaccess* we check the user object. If it is *NULL*, we simply set the request to forward back onto ourselves. Nothing is done in preDispatch if the action is already *noaccess*.

```
public function noaccessAction() {
    $data = array('username'=>'', 'password'=>'');
    $this->_initLayoutMessages('adminhtml/session');
    $block = $this->getLayout()->createBlock('adminhtml/template')
            ->setTemplate("$tplName.phtml");
    foreach ($data as $index=>$value) {
        $block->assign($index, $value);
    }
    $this->getResponse()->setBody($block->toHtml());

}
```

The contents of noaccessAction are taken from the Adminhtml module's IndexController as a way to easily show the login.phtml file. Now, showing the login page may not result in a proper XML document for our clients as much as showing an exception stack trace, but we can display any sort of template file we want here. We can even skip templating all together an output an XML message or call $this->echoXmlString('no access') and be done with it. Showing a complete HTML page to a hapless end-user that stumbled onto our AdminRest module via a browser would probably be more user friendly than showing XML output.

Client Access

Now that we have completed our simple order CRUD controller, we need to access it. Making your client log-in to the system is probably the most challenging part. It seems that simply posting login information an HTTP library, like cURL, is not sufficient to initialize a session. The specific steps involved to login to the admin are:

- Hit the login page to get a session cookie

- Save the cookies from the Set-cookie response header

- POST login[username] and login[password] to index.php/admin

- GET the URL index.php/admin (this triggers a redirect to the dashboard

- GET or POST to the CRUD API: index.php/adminrest/order/read

- Log out by request: index.php/admin/index/logout

The code, using the *Cognifty* HTTP library, looks like this:

```
Cgn::loadLibrary('Http::lib_cgn_http');

//get a cookie
$http = new Cgn_Http_Connection($ip,
        $url.'index.php/adminrest/order/read',
        $scheme,
        $port);
$http->setMethod('get');
$http->fetch();
list($cookie,$junk) = explode(';',
        $http->responseHeaders['Set-Cookie']);

$http = new Cgn_Http_Connection($ip,
        $url.'index.php/admin/', $scheme, $port);
$http->setMethod('post');
$http->setHeader('Cookie', $cookie);
$http->setHeader('Content-Type',
        'application/x-www-form-urlencoded');
$http->setBody(urlencode('login[username]').
        '=admin&'.urlencode('login[password]').'=password');
$http->fetch();

$http = new Cgn_Http_Connection($ip,
        $url.'index.php/admin/', $scheme, $port);
$http->setMethod('get');
$http->setHeader('Cookie', $cookie);
$http->fetch();

$http = new Cgn_Http_Connection($ip,
        $url.'index.php/adminrest/order/read', $scheme, $port);
$http->setMethod('get');
$http->setHeader('Cookie', $cookie);
$http->fetch();
if ( strlen($http->responseBody) ) {
    try {
        $xml = new SimpleXMLElement($http->responseBody);
    } catch (Exception $e) {
        //  die("BAD XML: ".htmlentities($http->responseBody));
        return false;
    }
}
```

What you do with the XML after you get it out is up to you and your specific needs. If you are connecting Magento to an order fulfillment system, ERP, or accounting package you will probably want to update the order's status to "processing" after each order is successfully inserted.

Some general ideas for integration include:

- Push the order into Mantis BT for tracking and alerts.

- Feed the data into an RSS stream (this was added to Magento 1.0)

- Scan the order for products that require attention.

- Push the order to different suppliers based on the items ordered

- Scan for fraudulent orders (high totals, ship to P.O. Boxes, etc)

- Insert the order into an order fulfillment system or accounting package

Hopefully you have seen the basics of getting order data out of Magento's back-end and into your developer hands as XML. With this information you can customize a solution to your organization's specific needs.

Chapter 11

Quick Answers to Common Questions

Magento's naming conventions are crazy!

Yes, they are. But there is a pattern to them. Whenever you see something in like `module/some_thing` that string directly translates into a class name. The only problem is, one of the pieces is missing. The missing piece is determined from the context, or reason, for getting the class. Here is the basic pattern:

```
"module/package_classname"

This translates into:

Mage_Module_???_Package_Classname

The ??? can only be known based on the context.
```

So, it can be said that `mage/package_classname` doesn't refer to anything unique, it could be one of a number of classes. This is true. But, we know from the basic structure of a module, that the only sub-directories available to us are:

- Model

- Controller

- Helper

- Block

So, the resulting class can only be one of those four, and it's not `Controller`. Controllers are special cases and don't follow the normal naming conventions. The context may or may not be readily apparent, but as you become more experienced with Magento the context will be apparent. Let's look at some examples and see the different contexts.

```
$product = Mage::getModel('customer/address');
//Translates into Mage_Customer_Model_Address

$url = $this->helper('customer')->getLoginPostUrl();
//Translates into Mage_Customer_Helper_Data  ("/data" is appended
   by default to helpers)

$url = $this->helper('giftmessage/url')->getSaveUrl();
//Translates into Mage_Giftmessage_Helper_Url

<block type="catalog/product_list" name="product_list"
      template="catalog/product/list.phtml" />
<!-- Even XML translates into Mage_Catalog_Block_Product_List -->
```

How do I run a raw query against the database?

First, you need a resource model, then you need a database connection from that resource model. After that, you are dealing with a simple Varien PDO Adapter (`Varien_Db_Adapter_Pdo_Mysql`) object, which is just a sub-class of `Zend_Db_Adapter_Pdo_Mysql`.

```
$w = Mage::getResourceSingleton('core/resource')->getConnection('core_write');
$result = $w->query('select 'entity_id' from 'catalog_product_entity');
if (!$result) {
  return false;
}
```

```
$row = $result->fetch(PDO::FETCH_ASSOC);
if (!$row) {
  return false;
}
```

How do I turn off the price in the layered navigation?

The idea here is that showing a breakdown of prices doesn't make sense to the end-user so you want to get rid of the price filter. This may not make sense to a customer of your site if you don't offer competing products, such as different sized air filters. You, as a customer, need to order a filter of a certain size to fill a certain sized hole in your furnace, comparing prices would probably end up only showing you filters that are too large or too small.

The price filter is constructed of *blocks*, specifically `Mage_Catalog_Block_Layer_View`. The price filter is some rendered HTML from a **model**, not from another block. The HTML specifically for the prices and categories are simply a list of items, so the rendering happens inside a model that contains the logic for splitting up the prices of all the products into groups. Then, these items are passed up to the specific block and end up as a *child* of `Mage_Catalog_Block_Layer_View`. We can easily remove this child with an `unset*()` call. A downside of this solution is that all the logic of the price filter still happens, the results are just thrown away.

- Edit your `app/design/frontend/yourstyle/yourtheme/layout/catalog.xml`

- Find the tag `<catalog_category_layered>`

- Add a tag under `<block type="catalog/layer_view` (this means break the self-closing syntax)

- Add an action tag, `method="unsetChild"`

- Alter some core code to throw away non-objects

```
<catalog_category_layered>
    <reference name="left">
        <block type="catalog/layer_view" name="catalog.leftnav"
            after="currency" template="catalog/layer/view.phtml">
        <!-- this is what was added -->
        <action method="unsetChild">
            <name>price_filter</name>
        </action>
        </block>
    <!--  ^^ remember to add a closing tag to this block tag -->
    </reference>
```

Since Magento's 1.0 release, you will now have to alter the behavior of the core block catalog/layer_view so that it doesn't try to work with non objects as if they were filters.

```
in Mage/Catalog/Block/Layer/View.php around line 135 make the foreach loop look
    like this:

        foreach ($filterableAttributes as $attribute) {
            $x =  $this->getChild($attribute->getAttributeCode().'_filter');
            if (is_object($x) ) {
                $filters[] = $x;
            }
            unset($x);
        }
```

How do I move the admin panel to a new name for security?

Let's say that you want to change the default URL of example.com/**admin**/ to example.com/**backend**/ to avoid any unwanted snooping around on your Web site. The only thing you have to do is adjust the Adminhtml module's **front-Name** so the router will match up the new URL to the module. Edit the /Mage/Adminhtml/etc/config.xml like so:

```
<config>
...
    <admin>
        <routers>
```

```
            <adminhtml>
                <use>admin</use>
                <args>
                    <module>Mage_Adminhtml</module>
                    <frontName>backend</frontName>
                </args>
            </adminhtml>
        </routers>
    </admin>
...
</config>
```

Make sure you disable the system's cache **before** you make this change, other wise you might get locked out of your admin pages.

If you don't like modifying the core code, you can create a shell module and make this XML the only part of your new module's config.xml file. Then, you simply enable your new module in app/etc/modules/*.xml. Look at the other XML files in that directory for examples of enabling modules.

How do I use installation and upgrade files in my custom modules?

Magento automatically installs or upgrades any module that it encounters during runtime. The installation files are located under **YourModule**/sql/**yourmodule**_setup/mysql4-install-**X.Y.Z**.php. The trigger for running this file is that your module's version number is not present in the DB table core_resource *and* that you have defined a version number in your module's etc/config.xml file. You will also need to define a global resource for your module's setup, use a tag name of <yourmodule_setup>. Without the resource definition that includes both setup module and a connection, the installation or upgrade will not perform, even if you increase the version number.

```
etc/config.xml contents...
<?xml version="1.0"?>
<config>
  <modules>
    <Company_YourModule>
      <version>0.9.12</version>
```

```
      </Company_YourModule>
    </modules>
    <global>
      <resources>
        <yourmodule_setup>
          <setup>
            <module>Company_YourModule</module>
          </setup>
          <connection>
            <use>core_setup</use>
          </connection>
        </yourmodule_setup>
      </resources>
    </global>
  </config>
```

Given that XML file, and an absence of any record containing company_yourmodule in table core_resource, your module's install file will be run the next time that module is executed.

Once installed, upgrades can be triggered when you change the version number in the XML configuration file to be greater than the value in core_resource. This will trigger a succession of any mysql4-upgrade-**X.Y.Z**.php file that has a version number greater than the number found in the core_resource table.

The syntax of these installation files looks like this:

```
$installer = $this;
/* @var $installer Mage_Catalog_Model_Resource_Eav_Mysql4_Setup */

$installer->startSetup();
$installer->run("
ALL YOUR SQL IN ONE STRING (the system breaks apart the SQL by semi-colon);
USE '{$installer->getTable('my_own_table')}' TO KEEP TABLE PREFIXES
    CONSISTENT;
");

$installer->endSetup();

/*
$installer->installEntities(); //only needed if you are installing
    new entities and they are defined properly
*/
//any other setup code such as inserting default data, caching data, etc.
```

How do I run Magento code without building a module?

Sometimes, running update scripts to quickly update the database or to export some data does not require a complete module to hold the code. For these types of operations you can build a shell script to get into Magento's environment without executing a traditional browser based request. The file is basically the Magento index.php file with one major change, instead of Mage::run('default') we will simply use Mage::app('default'). This type of file can be used to export pending orders, update product categorization, change available quantities, or any other type of automated maintenance.

```php
<?php
//if you store this script outside the Web site document
//  root (recommended) use chdir() to move execution back to
//  the document root.
//chdir("../magento/');

//if you are performing admin tasks, sometimes the system
//  checks if you are in SSL mode.  Uncomment the following
//  line to get this behavior.
//$_SERVER['SERVER_PORT'] = 443;

require_once 'app/Mage.php';
umask(0);
Mage::app('default');

//add your own code below:
/*
Example code:
load a category
$category = Mage::getModel('catalog/category')-load(1);

get a database handle
$w = Mage::getResourceSingleton('core/resource')->getConnection('core_write');
$w->query('select 'entity_id' from 'catalog_product_entity');
*/

?>
```

How do I show the root catalog category on the home page?

Currently, there is no way to signal which category that the `catalog/category_view` block acts on. The only way is by setting a category object in the `Mage::registry()`, and since the layout XML only works on Block objects, there is no way to affect the registry. You must alter (by re-writing or by overriding) the `getCurrentCategory()` method of the `Catalog/Block/Category/View.php` class.

```
/**
 * Retrieve current category model object
 *
 * @return Mage_Catalog_Model_Category
 */
public function getCurrentCategory()
{
    $_currentCategory =  Mage::registry('current_category');
    if (isset($_currentCategory)){
        return $_currentCategory;
    } else {
        $categoryId = (int)Mage::app()->getStore()->getWebsite()->
            getDefaultGroup()->getData('root_category_id');
        $category = Mage::getModel('catalog/category')->load($categoryId);
        Mage::register('current_category', $category);

        return $category;
    }
}
```

Now you are able to edit the home page in the *CMS > Manage Pages* link of the admin control panel. Change the *Layout Update XML* to this:

```
<reference name="content">
  <block type="catalog/category_view" name="category.products"
      template="catalog/category/view.phtml">
    <block type="catalog/product_list" name="product_list"
        template="catalog/product/list.phtml" />
  </block>
</reference>
```

Now, the home page will load the regular category view block, and when it tries to load the current category from the Mage registry, it will fail and find the current site's configured `root_category_id` and load that category instead. You could also add a simple `setCurrentCategory()` to this block class and pass it any ID you want from the layout XML.

If you know the exact category ID that you want to show, you can skip the above code and simply use this as the *Layout Update XML* for the home CMS page:

```
<reference name="content">
  <block type="catalog/product_list" name="product_list"
    template="catalog/product/list.phtml" >
    <action method="setCategoryId"><id>3</id></action>
  </block>
</reference>
```

How do I hide the price of products before they go into the cart or if a person is not logged in?

There are two places where the prices are formatted for display to the end user. The *catalog* (category view, and product view) and the *cart*. On the cart, one method is used for showing all the prices, including sub-total, tax totals, and the grand total, so it can be handled separately from the catalog's price formatting method. Both methods are *helpers* so we will override the two helpers and make sub classes in our own module.

For the checkout page, the helper is the default *Data* helper; for the catalog the helper is the *Product* helper class. The `config.xml` settings to override a helper are detailed below:

```
<config>

...
<global>
...

    <helpers>
      <catalog>
        <rewrite>
          <product>Company_YourModule_Helper_Product</product>
        </rewrite>
```

```
        </catalog>
        <checkout>
          <rewrite>
            <data>Company_YourModule_Helper_Checkout</data>
          </rewrite>
        </checkout>
      </helpers>

...
</global>
...
</config>
```

Now, we can make very small sub-classes of these base classes and change the methods in question.

```php
class Company_YourModule_Helper_Product extends Mage_Catalog_Helper_Product {
    /**
     * Overridden to hide price from anonymous users.
     *
     * @param   Mage_Catalog_Model_Product $product
     * @param   bool $displayMinimalPrice
     * @return  string
     */
    public function getPriceHtml($product, $displayMinimalPrice = false)
    {
        $loggedIn = Mage::getResourceSingleton('customer/session')->isLoggedIn()
            ;
        if (! $loggedIn ) {
            return "You must be logged into to see the price.";
        }
        return parent::getPriceHtml($product, $displayMinimalPrice);
    }
}
```

And the Checkout helper:

```php
class Company_YourModule_Helper_Checkout
    extends Mage_Checkout_Helper_Data
{
    /**
     * Overridden to hide price from anonymous users.
     */
```

```
    public function formatPrice($price)
  {
      $loggedIn = Mage::getResourceSingleton('customer/session')
         ->isLoggedIn();
      if (! $loggedIn ) {
        return "N/A";
        //return "You must be logged into to see the price.";
      }
      return parent::formatPrice($price);
  }
}
```

Notice how we can change the name of the helper from **Data** to **Checkout**, our own class names do not have to directly follow the same patterns as the default class names.

How do I find out the proper table name?

The core resource model has a method to get you any table name for any model in the system. Table names do not have to follow the name of the model, an end-user can change the table names by changing an XML setting. Also, any installation can have an arbitrary prefix for any table. Therefore, it is best to use the getTable method of the core resource.

```
$r = Mage::getResourceSingleton('core/resource')->getConnection('core_read')
$tableName = $r->getTable('catalog/product');
$tableName === 'catalog_product_entity';
```

This happens because we have the following XML configuration in the *catalog* module's config file.

```
<global>
   <models>
      <catalog>
         <class>Mage_Catalog_Model</class>
         <resourceModel>catalog_resource_eav_mysql4</resourceModel>
      </catalog>

      <catalog_resource_eav_mysql4>
```

```
<class>Mage_Catalog_Model_Resource_Eav_Mysql4</class>
<entities>
    <product>
        <table>catalog_product_entity</table>
    </product>
...
```

How do I show Magento products on a non-Magento page?

This is an often requested feature. There are a number of ways to do it too. You could create a listener to publish a category of products to static HTML whenever a category changes. You could run a cron script or other scheduled task to run some Magento code to export a category of products to a static file as well. The quickest way to get the job done is to simply include the necessary Magento files in your other PHP script and call the display logic.

Start with the basic shell magento script.

```
require_once '/path/to/app/Mage.php;

umask(0);
//not Mage::run();
Mage::app('default');
```

Assuming we want to display an entire category of products, we need to load up the category display block and render it. This will load the products and push the data through the associated template file.

```
//code snipped
$className = Mage::getConfig()
            ->getBlockClassName('catalog/product_list');
$block = new $className();

$className = Mage::getConfig()
             ->getBlockClassName('core/template');
$toolbar = new $className();
$block->setChild('toolbar', $toolbar);

//choose whatever category ID you want
```

```
$block->setCategoryId(3);
$block->setTemplate('catalog/product/list.phtml');
echo $block->renderView();
```

You might think that we would be using the *category view* block for this task, but we're not. The *product list* block is the component which does the actual printing of the products. The category view block does too much work preparing the rest of the page and is too integrated into Magento to cleanly use outside of Magento's code.

The reason that we make a `core/template` type block and call it "toolbar" is because the template file for the product list wants to show the output from a block called `toolbar`. If we set the real toolbar (type catalog/product_list_toolbar) then we start unraveling a whole lot of Magento dependencies, as the toolbar requires a product collection. This is the simplest, quickest way to render a category of products "outside" Magento.

Help, my product changes don't show up on the frontend!

Recently, this issue has come up for some users. When they make changes in the admin to certain products, the changes don't show up on the front end. This is most likely related to an incorrect *website id*. We haven't discussed multiple Web site support in this book as it isn't completely finished yet.

If you have this problem there is one simple solution that works most of the time. In the administrative backend, go to the *Manage Products* page. You should see a grid of products with a column of checkboxes on the left. This product grid is called a "mass update grid" because it can perform operations on any product you check-off. Select the problematic products by checking them. In the header bar for this grid, on the right, there should be a drop-down box with *Actions* next to it. Choose *Change Status*, then select *Enable* in the new status box that appears. Click the *submit* button to simply re-enable all of the problem products. This seems to work for most people.

I give up! Magento is too confusing

I hear you. Magento can certainly be overwhelming at times. Although it has some quirks, and some people feel it is over-engineered, you **can** get done what you want to get done. It's just PHP, after all.

The best advice I have if you're stuck is to simply make a copy of the `index.php.sample` file, call it whatever you want. Change the line with `Mage::run()` to `Mage::app()` and start trying out code samples below that line. The function `Mage::app()` simply initializes the entire Magento framework, but does not execute any request. This allows you to test any code you want in this file. You'll be able to figure out the problem if you just isolate your code troubles into a separate environment, like this sample file, and just keep plugging away at it.

Index

CPSIA information can be obtained
at www.ICGtesting.com
Printed in the USA
FSOW03n0654101216
28196FS